THE LAW OF POLICING
2nd Edition

FEDERAL CONSTITUTIONAL PRINCIPLES

by Randy Means

LRIS PUBLICATIONS
PORTLAND, OREGON

Published by Labor Relations Information System
3021 NE Broadway
Portland OR 97232
503.282.5440
www.LRIS.com

THE LAW OF POLICING, 2ND EDITION. Copyright 2014 by Randy Means. All rights reserved. Printed in the United States of America. No part of this book may be used or reproduced in any manner whatsoever without written permission except in the case of brief quotations embodied in critical articles and reviews.

Means, Randolph B. 1949 -

ISBN 978-1-880607-28-2

Library of Congress Control No. 2013957603

TO KATHERINE

ACKNOWLEDGMENTS

First and foremost, I thank my wife Katherine for the strength and grace she has shown in her successful battle against life-threatening cancer and the effects of its treatment during the last four years. Her courage has been an inspiration to me and to everyone who understood her situation.

I thank Will Aitchison, Valerie Aitchison, Debbie Frields Denman, Marc Fuller, and Tanja Olson of Labor Relations Information System – all of whom were involved in the preparation of this book – for their professionalism and kindness.

I acknowledge and thank the two professionals who assisted with legal research. Attorney Pam McDonald, former law enforcement officer, felony investigator and eventually felony prosecutor then college teacher, was a huge help in first-round research. Police Officer Zachary Miller finished the job in grand fashion. He is a nearly ten-year veteran whose professional development allows him to teach law at a regional police academy as he pursues his law school education and continues his police career.

I thank Professors Arnold Loewy and William Murphy who taught me constitutional law and criminal procedure at the University of North Carolina School of Law 40 years ago. They were wonderful teachers and I made As in their classes. Their work caused my original interest in this subject matter and I am grateful.

I thank my friend and teacher Dennis Andrade, career criminal investigator and consummate police leader, who for more than 20 years patiently showed me what good police work looks like. Now, four more good friends lead my continuing education. Captain (ret.) Greg Seidel left the Petersburg (VA) Police Department to become Director of Training for our firm. He is the best-rounded law enforcement professional I have ever met and he teaches me daily. Lt. Brian Fitch, Ph.D. is a watch commander with the Los Angeles County Sheriff's Department and teaches in the psychology departments of California state universities, in a law school, and at the LAPD Academy. At least monthly, he takes time out to guide my professional development. Sgt. (ret.) Dennis Conroy, Ph.D. does likewise. He spent an extraordinary career as an officer and supervisor in the St.

Paul (MN) Police Department while also working as a clinical psychologist for law enforcement officers, their employers, and their families – work that he continues in his "retirement." Chief (ret.) Curtis Spears left the Los Angeles County Sheriff's Department as a chief of operations. Before that, he was head of Professional Standards and Training. For more than a decade, he and I have taught together many times each year and my exposure to him is a constant education. I profusely thank these exceptional individuals for the time and effort they so generously give to me.

When I first attended FBI Academy training for police legal advisers 30-plus years ago, I was taught the subjects of which I now write. My instructors were Dan Schofield and John Hall. They were great role models and I thank them.

Most importantly from a professional development perspective, I thank my three career-long mentors, Reece Trimmer, Bob Farb, and Bob Thomas. Their thinking has so affected mine over the years that today I am unable to tell exactly where theirs ends and mine begins. Certainly, some of my words in this text were originally theirs.

Reece Trimmer, now deceased, was a Harvard Law School graduate who himself taught at a fine law school and who devoted nearly four decades to the police legal field. He was my full-time mentor for the first three years of my career and to me he will always be the Dean of the school of police law.

Bob Farb, also a Harvard-educated attorney, is a long-tenured Professor of Public Law and Government at the University of North Carolina. For nearly 35 years, I have studied his books on police law. Eventually, at his request, I reviewed his police law texts prior to their publication in order to add what I could.

Bob Thomas has been a recognized leader in the police law profession since 1974. He has been my law partner for nearly 25 years. Before, for nearly ten years, he was my mentor and supervisor as we worked together as in-house counsel to a major city police department. His professional knowledge is just amazing and I thank him from the bottom of my heart for so long and so willingly making me the beneficiary of his trailblazing.

Last, and certainly not least, I thank the law enforcement officers throughout this land who steadfastly keep faith with their oaths of office. In their everyday actions, they resolutely support, uphold and defend the Constitution of the United States of America and form the first line of our national defense. It is my great honor and privilege to assist them in their noble endeavor.

ABOUT THE AUTHOR

Randy Means, a partner in the Charlotte-based Thomas & Means Law Firm, specializes entirely in police operations and administration and assists a broad national clientele. He also writes the law and risk management column for *Law & Order* magazine and heads quality assurance and curriculum development for The Response Network, the endorsed on-line training provider for the FBI National Academy Associates and the Commission on Accreditation of Law Enforcement Agencies. His work has been mentioned in the "Wall Street Journal," discussed on "60 Minutes" and utilized on both the Law Enforcement Training Network and the FBI Training Network.

He has conducted advanced law enforcement training in every state and has taught nearly a half-million police officials. Today, in addition to his legal training, he teaches principles of leadership in dozens of law enforcement agencies, academies and command colleges.

A former active-duty military officer, he served eventually as second-in-command of a small combatant naval vessel. Later, he graduated from the University of North Carolina School of Law and served as head of legal training for North Carolina's state law enforcement training center, coordinator of legal training for the North Carolina State Bureau of Investigation, and for nearly ten years Police Attorney for the City of Charlotte. Subsequently, for two decades, he was the primary legal and risk management instructor for the International Association of Chiefs of Police. For several years, he was head of its Legal Officers Section, the national association of police attorneys.

He has been a speaker at national annual conferences of the FBI National Academy Alumni Association (FBINAA), Labor Relations Information System (LRIS), International Law Enforcement Educators and Trainers Association (ILEETA), Southern Police Institute (SPI) Alumni Association, International Association of Chiefs of Police (IACP), Public Risk and Insurance Management Association (PRIMA), State Risk Manager's Association (STRIMA), Public Agency Risk Manager's Association (PARMA), National Association of State Personnel Executives (NASPE), National Association of Government Training and Development Directors (NAGTADD)

International Association of State Directors of Law Enforcement Standards and Training (IASDLEST), International Personnel Management Association (IPMA), National Association of Field Training Officers (NAFTO), National Intelligence Academy (NIA), International Association of Law Enforcement Planners (IALEP), American Society for Law Enforcement Training (ASLET), International Association of Arson Investigators, North American Wildlife Enforcement Officers Association, National Information Officers Association (NIOA), National Conference of State and Provincial Police Planning Officers, Mid-Atlantic Law Enforcement Executive Development (LEED) Conference, the California Association of Police Training Officers (CAPTO), and COPSWEST (California Peace Officers Association), as well as annual police chiefs and sheriffs conferences in dozens of states. He has taught for the British Columbia Police Complaint Commission, the Los Angeles County Police Chiefs Association, Northwestern University, the Southwestern Law Enforcement Institute and the Institute of Police Technology and Management at the University of North Florida.

He has done law enforcement training in every state and specialized, in-house liability management training for the Houston Police Department, the Los Angeles County Sheriff's Department, the Maricopa County Sheriff's Office, the San Diego County Sheriff's Department, the Phoenix Police Department, the Honolulu Police Department, the Las Vegas Metropolitan Police Department, the Tucson Police Department, the Detroit Police Department, the Oregon State Police, the Alaska State Troopers, the El Paso Police Department, Arizona POST, California POST, Nevada POST, the Colorado State Police, the New Jersey State Police, the Kansas Highway Patrol, the North Carolina Highway Patrol, the Utah Highway Patrol, the St. Louis County Police Department, the Fairfax County (VA) Police Department, the Florida Marine Patrol, the United States Park Police, and the Drug Enforcement Administration (DEA), among hundreds of others. He has conducted law enforcement and risk management training for dozens of insurance and risk management companies and pools from coast to coast and for hundreds of academies, state police chiefs associations and other institutional providers of law enforcement training.

PREFACE

This writing is no substitute for a scholarly treatise. It is certainly not comprehensive. Rather, it is intended as a comparatively short, easy-to-read guide to its subject matter. Its primary use may be by law enforcement officers and those who teach the law of policing and related liability. To the extent that it serves the many attorneys and others who seek to navigate these waters, that secondary benefit is welcome.

Because case discussions and citations may hinder the flow of reading and since any comprehensive research should be performed with benefit of treatises and computers in any event, case law coverage in this book is limited almost entirely to representative decisions of the United States Supreme Court and the federal courts of appeals. There are 13 federal courts of appeal. Twelve of them have geographical areas of responsibility and decide criminal and civil rights cases. A decision of such a federal appeals court is binding law only in the geographical area over which that court has jurisdiction. In other parts of the country, such a decision would be studied for its possible persuasive value. For the many who have not memorized the boundaries of the various federal circuits, a map is provided below.

Geographic Boundaries
of United States Courts of Appeals and United States District Courts

State appellate court decisions are far too numerous and varied to be approached meaningfully in this writing and, for several reasons, sometimes provide poor guidance on federal constitutional principles. Naturally, a state appeals court decision is of great concern to those in that state. Thankfully, there are writings in most states that put forward the state-based statutory and case law that must be considered in reaching appropriate policy and procedure. Advice of local counsel, ideally expert in police legal matters, is essential.

Hopefully, this book will be read by many non-lawyers. Because it contains hundreds of case citations, those uninitiated in legal research may want to know that a case citation refers first to the volume number in which a particular publisher places a case decision. Next, the publisher and possibly the series of the publication are identified. Third is the page number at which the case is found in the referenced volume. Last, in parentheses, is the year in which the decision was rendered and, in the case of a federal appeals court decision, its circuit number. [e.g., *United States v. McKoy*, 428 F.3d 38 (1st Cir. 2005)].

Throughout this book, a variety of citations to published authorities has been used. To assist you in locating these authorities, the following glossary provides the full names of publications which may have been referred to in the book. If you have difficulties locating a particular case, please contact Labor Relations Information System for information on how to find it. Use of computers in legal research may eliminate the need to actually handle the sometimes dusty books.

Abbreviation	Full Name
F.2d	Federal Reporter, Second Series
F.3d	Federal Reporter, Third Series
F. Supp.	Federal Supplement
F. Supp. 2d	Federal Supplement, Third Series
F. Supp. 3d	Federal Supplement, Third Series
S. Ct.	Supreme Court Reporter
U.S.	United States Reporter

WARNING

This writing is based on federal law. There may be state law in your jurisdiction that is more restrictive of police procedure and/or more expansive of police liability than is federal law. Advice of local legal counsel is essential and is recommended with respect to all matters discussed in this writing. No action, policy, or procedure should be undertaken solely in reliance on this publication.

TABLE OF CONTENTS

CHAPTER ONE

INTRODUCTION AND DEFINITIONS — 1
What Is A "Search"? — 4
What Is A "Seizure"? — 5
"Unreasonableness" And Its Consequences — 6
Notes — 8

CHAPTER TWO

SEIZURES AND NON-SEIZURES OF PERSONS VOLUNTARY CONTACTS, INVESTIGATIVE DETENTIONS, AND ARRESTS — 9

The Voluntary Contact — 11
    The "Objective" Test As To Whether A Contact Is Voluntary — 12
    Free To Leave Versus Free To Decline — 13
    What Is The Effect Of *Miranda* Warnings On Whether A Contact Is Voluntary? — 16

Investigative Stops And Arrests — 17
Is The Seizure An Investigative Stop Or An Arrest? — 17
    How The Duration Of The Seizure Affects Whether The Seizure Is An Investigative Stop Or An Arrest — 17
    How The Involuntary Movement Of The Detainee Affects Whether A Seizure Is An Investigative Stop Or An Arrest — 21
    How The Use Of Force And/Or Restraints Affects Whether A Seizure Is An Investigatory Stop Or An Arrest — 23

When "Unarrest" Is Necessary — 25
    "Seizures" And The *Miranda* Rule — 26
    Notes — 28

CHAPTER THREE

REASONABLE SUSPICION AND PROBABLE CAUSE 31

The Definition Of Probable Cause And Reasonable Suspicion 33
Establishing Probable Cause And Reasonable Suspicion 34
Conceptualizing Reasonable Suspicion And Probable Cause 35
Sources Of Information 37
Source Credibility: Why Should This Source Be Believed? 39
    Police Officers 39
    Concerned Citizens 40
    Criminal Informants 41
    Confidential Informants 42
    Anonymous Tips 43
Frequently Recurring Elements Of Probable Cause Or Reasonable Suspicion 45
    Geographical Location Of The Subject 45
    High Crime Area 45
    A Caution On The "High Crime Area" Factor 45
    Time Factor 46
    Sensory Perceptions 46
    Suspect And Criminal Description Similarities 47
    The Suspect's Observed Behaviors 47
    Knowledge Of A Subject's Criminal History Or Past Criminal Behavior 48
    Profiling 49
    Unusualness 49
    Uncooperativeness 50

Officers' Collective Knowledge	51
Notes	53

CHAPTER FOUR
VEHICLE STOPS AND SEARCHES — 55

Stopping A Vehicle	57
Checkpoints	57
Pretext (Dual Purpose Stops)	58
Expanding Traffic Stops To Investigate Other Matters	59
Actions Related To The Stop	61
Consent To Search	62
Frisk Of Vehicle For Weapons	64
Frisk Of Occupants	65
Search Incident To The Arrest Of A Vehicle Occupant	67
Carroll Search (Probable Cause Search)	69
Probable Cause Searches Of Containers Within Vehicles	72
Inventory Searches	74
Summary	75
Notes	77

CHAPTER FIVE
FORCED ENTRY INTO PRIVATE PREMISES — 79

Terminology	81
The General Rules For Searches Of Premises	81
Liability Warning	82

Reasonable Belief In Arrestee's Presence	82
Exigent Circumstances	83
Entry To Arrest	84
Entry To Preserve Evidence	86
Crime Scenes	86
Other Emergencies	88
If A Warrant Is Required, What Kind Of Warrant?	89
Police-Created Exigencies	90
Addresses On Arrest Warrants	92
The Knock, Announce And Wait Requirements	92
Protective Sweeps	94
Notes	95

CHAPTER SIX
MIRANDA WARNINGS AND WAIVERS — 97

The "Custody" Principle	100
What Is "Custody"?	101
Intent To Arrest	104
What Is "Interrogation"?	105
The *Miranda* Warning	106
Re-warnings	107
The *Miranda* Waiver	108
Exceptions To The *Miranda* Requirement	110
Volunteered Statements	111
Notes	112

CHAPTER SEVEN

THE RIGHT TO COUNSEL AND THE RIGHT TO REMAIN SILENT — 113

Right To Counsel Issues	116
What Rights Have "Attached"?	117
When The Right To Silence Attaches	117
When The *Miranda*-Based Fifth Amendment Right To Counsel Attaches	118
When The Sixth Amendment Right To Counsel Attaches	118
What Words Constitute The Assertions Of Rights By Suspects?	118
If An Attached Right Has Been Asserted, What Then?	119
Assertions Of The Right To Silence	120
Assertions Of The Sixth Amendment Right To Counsel	120
Assertions Of The *Miranda*-Based Fifth Amendment Right To Counsel	122
Initiation Of Case Discussion By The Suspect	124
What Constitutes A Valid Waiver Of Each Right To Counsel?	125
Summary	126
Assertion Of Right To Silence By In-Custody Suspect	126
Assertion Of *Miranda*-Based Fifth Amendment Right To Counsel By In-Custody Suspect	127
Assertion Of Sixth Amendment Right To Counsel Directly To, Or In The Presence Of, Police By Formally Charged Suspect	128
A Final Note – "Voluntariness" And Coerced Statements	129
Notes	132

CHAPTER EIGHT

SEARCHES OF PERSONS 133

Frisk Searches	135
Suspicion Factors For Frisk Searches	137
Specific Information	137
Visual Observations	137
Nature Of The Suspected Criminal Activity	137
Discovery Of Weapons	137
Officer Knowledge Of Area And/Or Groups	138
Suspect Behavior	138
Scope And Nature Of The Frisk Search	139
The "Plain Feel" Doctrine	140
Exigent Circumstances (Probable Cause) Searches Of Persons	141
Special Needs Searches	142
School Searches	142
Airport Searches	143
Searches Of Probationers And Parolees	144
Search Incident To Arrest	145
Scope Of Search Incident To Arrest	146
Motor Vehicles And Searches Incident To An Arrest	147
Search Incident To Change Of Custody Or Location	148
Strip Searches/Body Cavity Searches	148
Search And Inventory Of Personal Possessions Of A Person In Custody	149
Notes	151

CHAPTER NINE

NON-SEARCHES: OPEN FIELDS AND WOODS, AND ABANDONMENT — 153

Open Fields And Woods	155
Abandoned Personal Property	158
Abandonment Of Residential Property	158
Abandonment Of Vehicles	159
Trash, Garbage, And The Abandonment Rule	159
Abandonment By Verbal Or Non-Verbal Interaction	160
Notes	162

CHAPTER TEN

NON-SEARCHES: THE PLAIN VIEW DOCTRINE, SENSORY PERCEPTION AND ENHANCEMENT TOOLS — 165

The Plain View Doctrine	167
Sensory Perceptions	171
Sensory Enhancement Tools	173
General Notes On Surveillance, Enhancement Tools, And Electronic Eavesdropping	175
Summary	176
Notes	177

CHAPTER ELEVEN

CONSENT TO SEARCH — 179

Deception To Obtain Consent	181

Who Can Consent?	182
Consent Considerations Arising Out Of An Officer's Language	184
The Consent Itself	186
Notes	187

CHAPTER TWELVE
SEARCH WARRANTS — 189

Exceptions To The Warrant Requirement	191
The Benefits Of A Warrant	192
Definitions Of Key Terms	192
What Is A Search Warrant?	192
What Is A Seizure?	193
What Is A Search?	193
What Is Involved In Applying For A Search Warrant?	193
The Descriptions In A Search Warrant	193
The Probable Cause Statement	194
Why Should The Information Be Believed?	195
Corroboration	196
What Is Enough For Probable Cause?	196
Obtaining The Warrant	197
Search Warrant Execution	197
The "Look Right" Test	197
Jurisdictional Issues	198
Time Frames	198
Re-Check Of Probable Cause	198
Re-Check Description(s)	198
Knock And Announce Requirements	199
Wait Time After Knock And Announce	200

Is There A "Reading" Requirement?	200
"Outside" Assistance	200
Detaining And Restraining Persons Present During The Execution Of A Warrant	200
Protective Sweeps	201
Special Tools And Tactical Teams	201
Searches Of Persons Present	201
Media Involvement	202
Length Of Search	203
Securing The Premises	203
Care Of Evidence	203
"Return" Of Warrant	203
After-Action Reports	204
Notes	205

CHAPTER THIRTEEN

NON-TESTIMONIAL IDENTIFICATION PROCEDURES — 207

What Are Non-Testimonial Identification Procedures?	209
Non-Testimonial Evidence Gained Through A Search Incident To An Arrest	210
Body Searches	211
Non-Testimonial Identification Orders	211
Service Or Execution Of Non-Testimonial Identification Orders	212
Consent Or Search Warrants	213
Juveniles	213
Lineups And Photographic Arrays	213
When Does The Right To Counsel Attach During The Identification Process?	215
Impermissible Suggestiveness In A Lineup Or	

Photo Array	216
Show-Ups	217
Uncooperativeness	218
Notes	219

CHAPTER FOURTEEN

THE USE OF FORCE IN POLICE PROCEDURES — 221

The Fourth Amendment Standard Of "Objective Reasonableness"	223
Deadly Force	226
No Requirement Of Least Intrusive Alternative	230
Notes	

INDEX — 237

CHAPTER 1

INTRODUCTION AND DEFINITIONS

Naturally, it is critical that law enforcement officers know and follow the law. It would be ironic indeed if law enforcement work were to begin with a violation of the law. Law **enforcement**, then, is reason in itself for law enforcement officers to obey the law, most importantly, the supreme law of the land – the United States Constitution. The oath of office is another positive reason for police to remain mindful of the law. Most oaths of office involve promises that officers will "support, uphold and defend" the Constitution of the United States of America. Surely in that lofty promise there is a necessarily implied sub-promise – that officers themselves will not become knowing violators of the very instrument that they have so solemnly pledged to support, uphold and defend.

Beyond these positive reasons to obey the Constitution, there are several negative ones. It is a federal felony for a law enforcement officer to willfully violate the constitutional rights of a citizen. Also, officers may be sued civilly for constitutional rights violations. Of course, evidence which is the direct product of a violation of someone's constitutional rights cannot be used in a criminal prosecution against the person whose rights were violated. The suppression of such evidence is required by what is now known as the "exclusionary rule" or "fruit of the poisoned tree" doctrine. Last, and as might be expected given the matters explained above, law enforcement employers may take administrative disciplinary action against an officer who violates constitutional rights. So, for a variety of reasons positive and negative, it is imperative that officers keep up with the law, especially obligations created by the federal constitution.

This book examines certain aspects of what some lawyers would call "pre-arraignment criminal procedure," the law of criminal investigation and, in particular, what law enforcement officers can and cannot do under the United States Constitution. While some state law is more restrictive of police behavior than is the federal constitution, most are mirror images of federal principles. In fact, much state statutory law dealing with police investigation of crimes is an outgrowth of the "Model Code of Pre-Arraignment Criminal Procedure," which was born in the mid-1970s and was intended largely to guide state law onto path-

> **While some state law is more restrictive of police behavior than is the federal constitution, most are mirror images of federal principles.**

ways that would not offend emerging federal constitutional principles. State law may be more restrictive of police practices than the federal constitution but naturally it cannot allow practices that would violate the federal constitution. The starting point, then, in determining the legality of a police action is deciding whether it passes muster under the federal constitution. This book is devoted to exactly that. While some of this book studies interrogation practices and identification procedures, most of it deals with interpretation of the Fourth Amendment to the United States Constitution – the law of "search and seizure." Consequently, it begins with definitions of those two terms as used in Fourth Amendment constitutional law.

> *State law may be more restrictive of police practices than the federal constitution but naturally it cannot allow practices that would violate the federal constitution.*

What Is A "Search"?

The Fourth Amendment protects one's right to be secure in his "person," "house," "papers" and "effects" from unreasonable government-sanctioned searches and seizures. The determination of whether a "search" has occurred involves a two-part analysis of the action of the officer. The first question is, "Has the officer physically intruded upon one of the four specific areas designated as receiving protection under the Fourth Amendment?" If the answer to this question is "yes" then no further analysis need be conducted – a search has occurred. If the answer is "no," however, another question must be asked, "Has the officer intruded upon a reasonable expectation of privacy?" If the answer is "yes" then a search has occurred.

So, a search occurs whenever a law enforcement officer physically intrudes upon a constitutionally-protected area[1] or intrudes upon a reasonable expectation of privacy.[2] An intrusion upon a reasonable expectation of privacy may or may not be "physical." Merely looking in a window of a home is a search if it "intrudes" upon a reasonable privacy expectation. Secretly listening to or recording a conversation in which there is a reasonable expectation of privacy is a search.

However, if an officer walks by a car that is in a public place and looks into the car through the window, he has not conducted a search, since a person cannot reasonably expect privacy in what he knowingly exposes to public view. On the other hand, if an officer opens the trunk of a car and looks into the trunk, a search has occurred because the officer intruded into a zone where privacy can reasonably be expected. The fact that the officer may not have touched or moved any item in the trunk is irrelevant. Once the officer has intruded upon a reasonable expectation of privacy, he has conducted a search.

The Fourth Amendment requires that unless a valid consent has been obtained, a search must be justified either by a search warrant or some recognized exception to the search warrant requirement.

> Scenario #1 A police officer, after arresting John Smith, opens John's cell phone and scrolls through the text messages.
>
> Question: Has the officer conducted a search?
>
> Answer: Yes. A person generally does not expose to the general public the contents of his cell phone, therefore the officer intruded upon a reasonable expectation of privacy.

What Is A "Seizure"?

A seizure of a <u>person</u> occurs whenever a law enforcement officer uses force on someone or a person submits to an officer's "show of authority."[3] When an officer says or does things that would cause a reasonable person to feel that he or she is required to participate in a contact with the officer, that person has been "seized." So, if a uniformed officer approaches someone on a sidewalk and says "Hold up there…I need to talk to you," a reasonable person would feel he was being required to stop. Assuming the person does stop as instructed, a seizure has occurred. The constitutional implications of seizing someone are discussed in detail later.

A seizure of <u>property</u> occurs when an officer interferes meaningfully or significantly with another person's possessory interest in that property.[4] Requiring that someone hand over a weapon during a brief detention is not a seizure of constitutional implication because the "interference" with a "possessory interest" is not so significant as to invoke the Fourth Amendment. However, a non-consensual "pat-down" which might reveal the presence of that weapon would be a search, as explained above, and would require Fourth Amendment justification. Taking that same weapon (non-consensually) to the police department for "safekeeping" or for processing would be a seizure which also would require satisfaction of the Fourth Amendment requirement that searches and seizures be reasonable.

A good summary of these definitions is found in the Supreme Court's decision in *United States v. Jacobsen*, 466 U.S. 109 (1984).

> Scenario #2 A police officer notices an occupied vehicle stopped on the side of the road, and parks his marked patrol car directly behind that vehicle and activates all of his emergency lights. The officer walks up to the car and begins to speak with the occupants.
>
> Question: Has the officer seized the occupants of the vehicle?
>
> Answer: Yes. A reasonable person, upon seeing a police car with all of its emergency lights activated parking behind him, would presume that he is required to stop for the officer.

"Unreasonableness" And Its Consequences

The Fourth Amendment prohibits "unreasonable" searches and seizures.

The Fourth Amendment prohibits "unreasonable" searches and seizures. To be reasonable, searches and seizures must be justified by facts and/or circumstances suggesting the need for them – probable cause, for example. Without such justification, searches and seizures are unreasonable and therefore unconstitutional, and any evidence which is the direct product of a violation of someone's constitutional rights is inadmissible in a criminal prosecution of the person whose rights were violated. An officer who intentionally violates someone's constitutional rights is guilty of a federal felony, and civil lawsuits against police for alleged constitutional rights violations are now commonplace.

This book contains hundreds of examples of what federal courts find to be reasonable, and unreasonable, searches and seizures. In other portions of this book are discussions of the law of interview and interrogation – the *Miranda* Rule and interpretations of the Fifth and Sixth Amendments. We begin with the law of officer-citizen contacts, seizures and non-seizures of persons.

Civil lawsuits against police for alleged constitutional rights violations are now commonplace.

> Scenario #3 A police officer observes John Smith walking down the street. The officer walks up to John and tells him that he is going to search him. The officer does not have probable cause to do so. Upon searching John, the officer discovers a bag of marijuana in John's pocket. John is charged with possession of marijuana and the matter is set for trial.
>
> Question: Will the officer be allowed to use the marijuana as evidence against John?
>
> Answer: No. Since the officer did not have probable cause to search John, the search was unreasonable. The marijuana is the product of an unreasonable search and therefore cannot be used against John in the subsequent criminal trial.

NOTES

[1] *United States v. Jones*, 132 S. Ct. 945 (2011); *Florida v. Jardines*, 133 S. Ct. 1409 (2013).

[2] *Katz v. United States*, 389 U.S. 347 (1967).

[3] *California v. Hodari D.*, 499 U.S. 621 (1991).

[4] *Maryland v. Garrison*, 480 U.S. 79 (1987).

ID: 2

CHAPTER 2

SEIZURES AND NON-SEIZURES OF PERSONS VOLUNTARY CONTACTS, INVESTIGATIVE DETENTIONS, AND ARRESTS

The Fourth Amendment to the United States Constitution requires that all searches and seizures, including seizures of persons, be reasonable. Determining the reasonableness of a seizure involves balancing the individual's right to be free and left alone by police with the occasional need of law enforcement to interfere with privacy and freedom in order to investigate crime and enforce laws.

For purposes of federal constitutional law, officer-citizen contacts fall into one of three legal categories:

1. Voluntary Contacts.
2. Investigative Detentions ("*Terry* Stops").
3. Arrests.

Investigative detentions and arrests are "seizures"; voluntary contacts are not.

Courts may use different words to describe these interactions, but ultimately, there are only three categories. Officers are required to control a contact so that it does not escalate into an intrusion (seizure) for which the officer may not have legal justification. Before it can be determined what legal justification, if any, is required for an officer-citizen contact, it is necessary to determine what type of contact is taking place. In order to do that, one must know the characteristics of each type of contact.

> **Before it can be determined what legal justification, if any, is required for an officer-citizen contact, it is necessary to determine what type of contact is taking place.**

The Voluntary Contact

Where there is no "seizure" within the meaning of the Fourth Amendment, there is no Fourth Amendment requirement of "reasonable" factual justification for the contact. In a voluntary contact, because there is no seizure, police need not have or prove reasonable suspicion or probable cause. For that reason, among several other practical advantages, voluntary contacts tend to well serve the interests of police.

> Scenario #4 A police officer observes an occupied vehicle parked in a parking lot during broad daylight. The officer approaches the vehicle on foot, knocks on the window and asks the driver if he is willing to speak to him. The driver opens the door and says, "Sure. What's up?" The officer then immediately sees a bag of marijuana laying on the floor of the vehicle. The officer seizes the marijuana and the driver is arrested. During the criminal trial, the defense attorney demands the marijuana evidence be suppressed, claiming an illegal seizure of the defendant for lack of reasonable suspicion.
>
> Question: Was this contact a seizure of a person or a voluntary contact?
>
> Answer: The transaction began as a voluntary contact as the officer simply walked up to the car and asked the driver if he would be willing to speak with him. The marijuana sighting, then plain view seizure, was the product of that initial voluntary contact.

The "Objective" Test As To Whether A Contact Is Voluntary

Officer-citizen contacts are legally voluntary if, in view of all circumstances surrounding the transaction, a reasonable person would have believed he was free to leave and/or decline the contact with law enforcement officers. This test focuses on what officers have actually said and/or done, and how reasonable people would interpret those words and actions. According to the Supreme Court, "only when the officer, by means of physical force or show of authority, has restrained the liberty of a citizen may we conclude that a 'seizure' has occurred."[1]

The test for seizure of a person involves an objective standard – looking to a reasonable person's interpretation of police behavior rather than to the suspect's personal or subjective view of it. This standard ensures that the scope of an officer's Fourth Amendment authority does not vary with the state of mind of the particular individual approached by the officer. In *Florida v. Bostick*, 501 U.S. 429 (1991), the Supreme Court specified that the reasonable person is an innocent person and therefore presumably does not suffer guilt-induced paranoia every time police approach. An individual suspect may feel and may testify that he was detained or arrested at a given point in time, but unless the officer has said or done something that would cause a reasonable person to feel that way, no seizure has occurred.[2]

Whether the involved officer himself subjectively believed he was or was not seizing someone – and, if so, whether he was arresting or merely detaining him – is generally not relevant to the legal determination of whether a seizure has occurred. An officer may believe that his action in seizing a person was only an investigative detention, but a court may still decide that the objective facts showed that the officer's action was an arrest and therefore required probable cause.

> **Whether the involved officer himself subjectively believed he was or was not seizing someone is generally not relevant to the legal determination of whether a seizure has occurred.**

Scenario #5 John Smith is approached on a public street by a uniformed police officer. The officer asks John if he would be willing to speak with him. John, fearful and distrustful of the police, accepts because he feels that one cannot say no to police.

Question: Is this a voluntary contact or a seizure?

Answer: Though John did not feel that he could decline the officer's request, a reasonable person would feel free to decline because the officer said and did nothing to suggest that John was required to participate. Therefore, this was a voluntary contact.

Free To Leave Versus Free To Decline

Some have suggested that whether an officer-citizen contact amounts to a seizure depends upon whether the citizen is free to leave. This is a bit of an overstatement. While a "free to leave" inquiry is often determinative, it is not the sole test for whether an officer-citizen contact is a seizure. There are circumstances in which someone is not necessarily free to leave but the contact still might not be a seizure.

Suppose in an attempted armed robbery of a convenience store clerk, the clerk and gunman scuffle. The perpetrator fires but only wounds himself. He flees but police find his blood and obtain his physical description. Thirty minutes later, police learn that a person has arrived at a nearby hospital with a gunshot wound; he matches the description of the robbery suspect. Police go to the hospital and obtain permission from the emergency room doctor to speak with the suspect while he is awaiting treatment in an examination room. The doctor tells police that the subject has not received any medication and that his wound is superficial. There ensues the following conversation with the suspect:

> Officer: "Good afternoon. I'm Officer John Smith with the City Police Department. How are you feeling?"
>
> Suspect: "O.K. A few stitches and I'll be as good as new."
>
> Officer: "Great. Sir, may I have your permission to talk with you a moment? Would you allow me to do that?"
>
> Suspect: "Sure. No problem. What's up?"

In this scenario, the suspect arguably was not free to leave in that he was waiting in a hospital to receive treatment for his injury. Still, it appears he was free to decline the contact with the officer. Nothing in the officer's communication indicated otherwise. He asked the suspect to participate in the transaction; there were no words of command, demand, requirement, or instruction. Though the suspect may not have been "free to leave," circumstances indicated he was "free to decline" the contact with the officer. Therefore, the contact is not a seizure. The "free to decline" test has been applied by the United States Supreme Court in several cases.[3]

The "free to decline" test has been applied by the United States Supreme Court in several cases.

More frequently, however, the "free to leave" test will be sufficient to govern the categorization of the contact. Example: An officer observes a young man walking in an area where a number of burglaries have occurred recently. With no other specific information in mind, the officer approaches the citizen and says, "Excuse me, sir, may I speak with you for a moment?" The man stops and says, "Yeah, what is it?" The officer identifies himself and asks if he could see some identification, which the man agreeably produces. The officer asks a few questions, and the two part ways. Because the officer said and did nothing that would cause a reasonable person to feel restrained or otherwise required to participate in the contact, this contact is entirely voluntary in the legal sense.

The Supreme Court has held that if all a police officer does is approach a subject, identify himself or herself as a police officer, and ask, in a manner that suggests an option, to speak to the subject, a reasonable person does not feel restrained or required to participate in the transaction.[4] Of course, tone of voice and/or other conduct could change the result if used coercively. In *INS v. Delgado*, 466 U.S. 210 (1984), the Supreme Court held that law enforcement officers did not seize members of a factory workforce even though officers were stationed near exits while others approached and questioned the workers inside. A similar result occurred in *United States v. Ojeda-Ramos*, 455 F.3d 1178 (10th Cir. 2006), where the Court held that a passenger ordered (along with others) to leave a bus during a scheduled stop was not seized.

For an officer, the key to creating a voluntary contact is to request cooperation in a manner that suggests an option or simply to strike up a normal, non-coercive conversation. The officer's exact words are critical. The officer must request or invite the subject's participation, not order, demand, require, instruct, or otherwise coerce it. Evidence of the officer's exact words may include testimony by the officer, the subject, and other witnesses, as well as any recordings that may exist. Non-verbal communication will be relevant as well. While "kind tones" may help, they will not keep plain language from creating a seizure.[5]

The key to creating a voluntary contact is to request cooperation in a manner that suggests an option.

Scenario #6 A police officer, patrolling an apartment complex on foot, sees John Smith walking down the sidewalk. She approaches John and asks if she can talk to him. John replies, "No, thank you" and keeps walking. The officer follows John and repeats her request. John again responds negatively. The officer still follows and asks again for cooperation. John finally stops and honors the officer's request to speak with her.

SEIZURES AND NON-SEIZURES OF PERSONS — 15

> Question: Is this a voluntary contact or a seizure?
>
> Answer: This contact will likely be viewed as a seizure because a reasonable person would conclude that the officer was unwilling to take "no" for an answer.

What Is The Effect Of *Miranda* Warnings On Whether A Contact Is Voluntary?

In *Miranda v. Arizona*, 384 U.S. 436 (1966), the U.S. Supreme Court ruled that a person in police custody must be advised of certain rights and warned that anything he says prior to being interrogated by the police can be used against him. Among these rights is the right to refuse to answer any questions the police may ask and the right to have an attorney present during the questioning. The purpose of the *Miranda* warning is to ensure that any confession or other testimonial evidence obtained from the interrogation is not a product of the coercion inherently present in police custody.

Giving *Miranda* warnings may be counter-purposeful for the officer who is trying to achieve, and prove, that a subject has not been seized. Given that federal law requires *Miranda* warnings only in custodial interrogations, a reasonable person who is advised of *Miranda* rights might reasonably conclude that he is in custody, i.e., that he has been seized. To avoid this problem, some officers, instead of explaining custodial interrogation rights (*Miranda* rights) in a non-custodial setting, spend the same time explaining and assuring that the contact is in fact non-custodial. Example: "Billy, you are not under arrest and you're free to leave at any time. We're just asking for your voluntary cooperation. Would you be willing to discuss this matter with us?"

When circumstances would cause a reasonable person to feel that he is being subjected to restraints normally associated with an arrest, interrogative questions by police require prior warning and waiver of *Miranda* rights. Interrogation of a suspect without *Miranda* warning and waiver is permitted as long as officers have not said or done anything that would cause a reasonable person to feel that he is under arrest at the time of the questioning.[6]

Investigative Stops And Arrests

If an officer-citizen contact is a seizure within the meaning of the Fourth Amendment, it next must be determined what kind of seizure has occurred. There are two possibilities: arrest and investigative detention, or "stop." In this discussion, the terms "investigative detention," "detention," and "stop" are used interchangeably and have identical meanings. Such actions are also often called "*Terry* Stops," referring to *Terry v. Ohio,* 392 U.S. 1 (1968), the Supreme Court's landmark stop and frisk case.

Because investigative detentions and arrests are seizures, they implicate the Fourth Amendment and its "reasonableness" requirements. This means showing certain pre-existing levels of factual justification – reasonable suspicion for stops, probable cause for arrests. But how does one determine whether a seizure is a stop or an arrest?

Is The Seizure An Investigative Stop Or An Arrest?

Deciding whether a seizure is an investigative stop or an arrest requires a determination of "whether…arrest-like measures implemented can nevertheless be reconciled with the limited nature of a *Terry*-type stop."[7] Courts tend to isolate three issues in order to determine whether a seizure is "arrest-like" or "*Terry*-type": (1) The duration of the seizure; (2) whether the seized individual has been involuntarily moved from one place to another; and (3) whether physical force and/or restraints were used. Naturally, the words "you're under arrest" also would be determinative.

How The Duration Of The Seizure Affects Whether The Seizure Is An Investigative Stop Or An Arrest

Investigative detentions must be brief. Normally, issues involved in an investigative detention may be resolved in minutes (not hours) and should therefore be completed in that time. Stops of much more than an hour are likely to be re-categorized as arrests and would therefore require probable cause for their

Investigative detentions must be brief.

justification. For example, in *U.S. v. Codd*, 956 F.2d 1109 (11th Cir. 1992), the Court found that a two-and-a-half-hour detention went far beyond the boundaries of an investigative detention. In some cases, particularly serious ones where investigation is progressing efficiently toward a determination of presence or absence of probable cause, a detention of an hour or more may be reasonable and therefore constitutional.[8] In *U.S. v. Maltais*, 403 F.3d 500 (8th Cir. 2005), the Court held that a two-hour and 55-minute investigative detention was reasonable when officers diligently summoned a drug dog to a remote area near the Canadian border at 1:00 a.m., then awaited its arrival.

In *United States v. Sharpe*, 470 U.S. 675 (1985), the Supreme Court dealt with a case where law enforcement officers performing surveillance in an unmarked car developed reasonable suspicion that a particular pickup truck was illegally transporting drugs. A sedan was traveling in tandem with the truck. After following the vehicles for a number of miles, the officers decided to conduct an investigative stop and radioed another officer for assistance. When the officers attempted to stop the two vehicles, the sedan stopped but the truck continued with the newly-joined assisting officer following. The originally-involved officers talked with the sedan driver and, after first obtaining his driver's license, left the sedan and its driver with a fourth officer and began looking for the truck and the assisting officer. They found that the assisting officer had stopped the truck and detained its driver. Twenty minutes after the truck was stopped, the initiating officers arrived, put their noses against the rear window of the truck and smelled marijuana. The issue for the Supreme Court was whether the detection of the marijuana odor was part of a lawful investigative detention or had the stop at that point exceeded permissible time limits. The Court held that the truck transaction was a proper investigative detention because there was reasonable suspicion and the roughly 20-minute detention was reasonable. The detection of the odor of marijuana and consequent development of probable cause to search occurred during a period of lawful investigative detention. The probable cause to search justified the opening of the camper shell; the then-found drug evidence was therefore obtained lawfully.

Another Supreme Court decision involving time limits of investigative detention is *United States v. Place*, 462 U.S. 696 (1983). In that case, two officers on duty at a major airport approached a subject reasonably suspected of drug courier activity. The officers requested permission to search his luggage. Though the suspect consented to the search, the search was not conducted because the suspect's flight was about to leave. The officers called drug interdiction agents at the destination airport and informed them of the reasonable suspicion. Agents at the destination airport approached the suspect after he claimed his luggage. When the suspect refused to consent to a search of the bag, officers told him they were going to take his luggage and attempt to obtain a search warrant, and that he could accompany them if he desired. The suspect declined. They then took his luggage to another nearby airport where a trained narcotics detection dog was available to conduct a sniff test, which was positive for drugs. Approximately 90 minutes had elapsed between the time the bag was detained and the time of the sniff test. The subject was subsequently arrested for possession of cocaine. The issue for the Court was whether the detention of the luggage, which was based on reasonable suspicion, exceeded permissible time limits before the sniff test was performed and probable cause was established.

The Supreme Court concluded that the seizure of the bag exceeded permissible time limits for an investigative detention. The Court noted that the agents knew the suspect would be arriving at the destination airport and they could have and should have arranged for the dog to be at that location. By showing such concern over the 90-minute detention of a piece of luggage (with reasonable suspicion but not probable cause), the Court gave clear indication that the investigative detention of persons for such a period would be closely scrutinized and that investigative detentions must be limited to periods of diligent, active investigation. In less serious matters, even an hour could be too long for an investigative stop supported by less than probable cause. If initial investigation reveals the need for other or different investigation, the duration of the stop may sometimes be extended slightly.[9]

In less serious matters, even an hour could be too long for an investigative stop supported by less than probable cause.

Both *Sharpe* and *Place* involve investigative detentions that included an extended period of time during which the police were awaiting additional resources to arrive in order to proceed with the investigation. A common question the Court addressed in each was whether or not the police diligently pursued a means of investigation that was likely to confirm or dispel the suspicion. In *Sharpe*, the Court concluded that during the extended investigative detention the officers were, in fact, diligently pursuing the narcotics investigation. However in *Place*, the fact that it took an additional 90 minutes for the drug sniff dog to arrive at the destination airport demonstrated a lack of diligence on the part of the police. The police at the destination airport, upon receiving the imputed reasonable suspicion from the officers at the departing airport, should have made arrangements for the dog to be present when the plane arrived.

> Scenario #7 A police officer sees a man walking down the street that matches the description of a burglary suspect near enough to establish reasonable suspicion, so the officer detains him. The man denies any involvement in the burglary and there is no other evidence linking him to the crime. The officer, still having a gut feeling that this man is guilty of the burglary, decides that he is going to make the man "sweat it out a little bit" in hopes that he can get the man to confess. The officer has the man sit on the sidewalk for 15 more minutes and no further investigation is conducted.
>
> Question: Is the duration of this investigative detention reasonable?
>
> Answer: No. An investigative detention generally must be brief and may only continue so long as the investigation is progressing actively and diligently. In this case, waiting 15 minutes to pressure the subject is not an acceptable reason for prolonging the seizure.

How The Involuntary Movement Of The Detainee Affects Whether A Seizure Is An Investigative Stop Or An Arrest

Moving a suspect can affect whether a seizure is an investigative stop or an arrest. In *Florida v. Royer*, 460 U.S. 491 (1983), the Supreme Court ruled that the involuntary movement of a detained subject from an airport concourse to a small, police-controlled room 40 feet away, for purposes of facilitating a luggage search, created an arrest-like event that required pre-existing probable cause. As a plurality of the Court went on to explain: "There are undoubtedly reasons of safety and security that would justify moving a suspect from one location to another during an investigatory detention, such as from an airport concourse to a more private area."

Royer thus teaches that movement of a detainee even a short distance, in the absence of legitimate and articulatable safety and security justifications, may create an arrest requiring probable cause though the encounter only lasts a few minutes. Short movements within one environment for safety and security reasons may occur without creating an arrest. For example, see *United States v. $109,179 in U.S. Currency*, 228 F.3d 1080 (9th Cir. 2000), where a detained subject was moved from one motel room to another without creating an arrest at that point. But just stating that the movement was for "safety and security" may not suffice as the required articulation – the factual basis for the safety or security concern – must be stated.[10]

The *Royer* case raises another question. The officers approached a subject in an airport concourse because particular aspects of his conduct and demeanor were consistent with a drug courier profile. The officers identified themselves and asked if the subject had a moment to talk. He responded affirmatively. Officers then asked to see his airline ticket and some other form of identification, which he produced. His airline ticket was in the name "Holt" and his driver's license in the name "Royer." Asked to explain the two names, he became very nervous and failed to give a reasonable explanation. Officers then informed the subject that he was suspected of drug smuggling and, without returning his driver's license or ticket, asked him to accompany them to a room approximately 40 feet away. There, officers obtained consent to search his luggage. Drugs were found during the consent search. Was the consent search the product of a lawful investigative detention or an unlawful arrest?

The plurality opinion of the Court held that the evidence from the consent search was the product of a police action that was either an arrest or so arrest-like as to require pre-existing probable cause. Because there was not yet probable cause to arrest at the time the involuntary movement was undertaken, the resulting evidence was inadmissible. However, also as mentioned above, the Court noted that the result could have been different if the officers had explained in their testimony legitimate safety or security reasons for the short movement.

> **If there is not yet probable cause to arrest at the time the involuntary movement was undertaken, the resulting evidence is inadmissible.**

Two years later, in *Hayes v. Florida*, 470 U.S. 811 (1985), the Court again dealt with the issue of the involuntary movement of a suspect. Officers conducting a felony investigation had a principal suspect but insufficient evidence to arrest him. When latent prints were found in the victim's bedroom, officers decided to visit the suspect's home to obtain his fingerprints. They did not seek a court order authorizing this procedure. The suspect spoke with officers on the front porch of his home and told them he did not want to go to the police station for fingerprinting. An officer responded, "Sir, if you don't come with me, I will have to place you under arrest." The suspect replied, "In that case I will go." He was then taken to the police station and fingerprinted. Was the resulting fingerprint evidence the product of a lawful investigative detention or an unlawful arrest?

The Court held that the transaction was, in essence, an illegal arrest. The officer's method of getting the suspect to accompany him to the station was a seizure because a reasonable person would have felt that he was required to go with the officer. Because the seizure involved involuntary movement from place to place, it was sufficiently like an arrest as to require probable cause to arrest at that point. Evidence resulting from the seizure was product of an illegality – fruit of a poisoned tree – and was suppressed.

In *Kaupp v. Texas*, 538 U.S. 626 (2003), the Court restated its view that involuntary movement of a seized person to another place is, in essence, an arrest. Importantly, *Hayes* and *Kaupp*, as well as the earlier case of *Dunaway v. New York*, all involved requiring a person to accompany police to a law enforcement facility.[11] Only *Royer* involved movement to some other place. Lower courts are split, as was the *Royer* court, on whether requiring a detained person to move to a non-police dominated location would be an arrest (for example, moving someone from one public location to another public location). Some courts have held that moving a detained person to another nearby location for a one-on-one identification, or show-up, is not an arrest.[12] Because of confusion in this area of the law, the better course may be for officers to have the eyewitness come to the place of the detention or take a digital photo and transmit it to an officer with the eyewitness, rather than require the detainee to go to the location of the eyewitness.

> *Lower courts are split on whether requiring a detained person to move to a non-police dominated location would be an arrest.*

Scenario #8 An officer approaches a man sitting on the edge of a long pier. The man is yelling incoherently and the officer has reason to believe that he may be under the influence of some type of drug. The officer tells the man that, for the safety of them both, he needs to come with the officer to the shore so that he may continue his investigation. The officer takes hold of the man's arm and escorts him to the shore.

Question: Has the involuntary movement of the man transformed this investigative detention into an arrest?

Answer: No. The officer has a legitimate safety concern and moving the investigation a short distance to the shore is reasonable under these circumstances.

How The Use Of Force And/Or Restraints Affects Whether A Seizure Is An Investigatory Stop Or An Arrest

Non-deadly force and other restraints may be used as reasonably necessary to effect and safely maintain an investigative detention; such actions do not automatically convert the transaction into an arrest. In fact, in *Terry v. Ohio*, 392 U.S. 1 (1968), the Supreme Court's original "stop and frisk" case, the Court approved the seizure of a person on less than probable cause where a police officer "grabbed [a subject] and spun him around" before proceeding with a frisk.

In a variety of lower court decisions, courts have held the use of reasonable force in investigative stops, up to and including stops conducted at gunpoint, does not necessarily convert a detention into an arrest, as long as there is strong justification for the force or show of force.[13] Similarly, blocking an escape path, handcuffing and/or locking the suspect in a police vehicle may be appropriate in some investigative detentions where reasonably necessary to ensure officer safety or security of the detainee.[14]

Thus, an officer may use force as reasonably necessary – including touching, grabbing, or pointing a gun – in order to stop a person. However, if there is more force than reasonably necessary, a court may determine that what would otherwise have been considered an investigative stop was in fact an arrest and therefore required pre-existing probable cause.[15]

Scenario #9 A police officer responds to the area of a reported armed robbery that just occurred. He had been told that the described suspect pointed a handgun at the victim and demanded his money. Upon arrival in the area, the officer observes an individual that very closely matches the description of the suspect – enough so for reasonable suspicion. The officer approaches the individual, draws and points his service pistol at the individual, orders him to the ground and handcuffs him. The officer tells the suspect that he is not under arrest but that he is being temporarily detained.

Question: Was the officer's use of force reasonable in the context of this investigative detention or did his use of force render the encounter an arrest?

Answer: Given the fact that he encountered this suspect in close proximity to the scene of a violent crime involving the use of a firearm, his use of his service weapon in this manner was reasonable and did not morph the detention into an arrest.

When "Unarrest" Is Necessary

Perhaps the strange word "unarrest" should be replaced with a phrase that sounds more "legal": "Discontinuation of arrest custody upon dissipation and/or evaporation of probable cause." In any event, it is the view of many police law experts that if, after making an arrest, an officer discovers that probable cause did not exist in the first place or has now evaporated, the subject should be released as quickly as possible. This would occur, ideally, in a safe place, preferably of the arrestee's choosing. It is not necessary or desirable that the arrestee be further processed or presented to a judicial official. Instead, the details of the arrest and unarrest should be thoroughly documented, along with the justifications for each. A compelling argument exists that continued custody after the evaporation of probable cause for an arrest violates the Fourth Amendment. On such facts, "unarrest" may be constitutionally imperative.[16] This may be true notwithstanding a state statute that might read something like "upon making an arrest, the officer shall present the arrestee to a judicial officer without unnecessary delay." Such statutes exist to assure proper handling of people who are being kept in custody, not those being released from it.

If, after making an arrest, an officer discovers that probable cause did not exist in the first place or has now evaporated, the subject should be released as quickly as possible.

Scenario #10 After conducting field sobriety tests, a police officer arrests a man for drunk driving and transports him to the police station to have the suspect provide a breath sample. The result of the breath test, conducted 30 minutes after the arrest, is 0.01. State law dictates that a person with a blood alcohol concentration of 0.01 is considered to be "not under the influence of alcohol." The officer has no reason to suspect that the man is under the influence of any other substances.

Question: What should the officer do?

Answer: The officer should promptly "unarrest" the suspect. The officer had probable cause to arrest the man at the scene but the probable cause was negated by the results of the breath test. Continued custody would violate the Fourth Amendment.

"Seizures" And The *Miranda* Rule

Although the *Miranda* rule is discussed in more depth later, it should be noted here that one consequence of the categorization of an officer-citizen contact is its effect on whether or not *Miranda* warning and waiver procedures are required prior to questioning of the subject. Ironically, the simplest part of the *Miranda* rule is the most frequently misunderstood. The rule applies only when a person is interrogated while in police "custody."[17] The test for *Miranda* "custody" is objective: Would a reasonable person feel that he was subjected to restraints normally associated with formal arrest? The subjective feelings of a particular subject are of no consequence in deciding whether the subject is in custody for *Miranda* purposes. The question is: Has the officer said and/or done things that a reasonable person normally associates with being arrested?[18] When a subject comes to and remains at the interrogation site on a voluntary basis there is no *Miranda* custody, even when suspicion is "focused" and there is accusatory interrogation.[19] A roadside stop (investigative detention) is not "custody" for purposes of *Miranda*, but an arrest is.[20] Custody, not focus of suspicion, determines whether a person to be interrogated is entitled to *Miranda* warnings.[21] The concept of "custody" for purposes of *Miranda* is almost identical to the Fourth Amendment concept of "arrest" but is slightly broader. It includes those investigative detentions that are so arrest-like that reasonable people could mistake them for an arrest. Gun pointing, handcuffing, and locking someone in the back of a police car may all be reasonable parts of some *Terry* stops, but those measures could easily be viewed by a reasonable person as the beginning of an arrest. Consequently, they may also signal the beginning of *Miranda* custody.

When an officer is trying to assure a non-custodial environment, it is generally useful to remind people that they are not under arrest, that they are free to leave and that the officer is seeking their voluntary participation. In cases where a subject has been detained (but not arrested), the officer may wish to explain that status to him as well – in order to assist with a proper characterization of the transaction later in court.

Scenario #11 A police officer sees a man walking down the street that very closely matches the description of a burglary suspect. An investigative detention is reasonable. The officer walks up to him and tells him he is being detained for questioning. No force or restraints are used by the officer.

Question: Is the officer required to give this man a *Miranda* warning prior to questioning him?

Answer: No. Though the man has been detained, he has not been subjected to any restraints normally associated with a formal arrest (i.e. handcuffs, placing in the back of a patrol car, pointing of a weapon, etc.) and is not in "custody" for purposes of *Miranda*.

NOTES

[1] *California v. Hodari D*, 499 U.S. 621 (1991).

[2] *See, for example, United States v. Al Nasser*, 555 F.3d 722 (9th Cir. 2009).

[3] *See, e.g., United States v. Drayton*, 536 U.S. 194 (2002); *Florida v. Bostick*, 501 U.S. 429 (1991); *INS v. Delgado*, 466 U.S. 210 (1984).

[4] *See*, for examples, the *Drayton, Bostick*, and *Delgado* decisions, above, as well as *Florida v. Royer*, 460 U.S. 491 (1983).

[5] *See United States v. Richardson*, 385 F.3d 625 (6th Cir. 2004).

[6] *Berkemer v. McCarty*, 468 U.S. 420 (1984); *Stansbury v. California*, 511 U.S. 318 (1994). [NOTE: The law of interrogation, including *Miranda* principles, is covered more thoroughly starting at page 105]

[7] *United States v. Acosta-Colon*, 157 F.3d 9 (1st Cir. 1998).

[8] *See United States v. Gil*, 204 F.3d 1347 (11th Cir. 2000)(75 minutes) and *United States v. McCarthy*, 77 F.3d 522 (1st Cir. 1996)(also 75 minutes) as examples.

[9] *See, e.g., United States v. Soto-Cervantes*, 138 F.3d 1319 (10th Cir. 1998)(one-hour stop permitted).

[10] *United States v. Acosta-Colon*, 157 F.3d 9 (1st Cir. 1998).

[11] *See Dunaway v. New York*, 442 U.S. 200 (1979).

[12] *See, e.g., United States v. McCargo*, 464 F.3d 192 (2d Cir. 2006); *United States v. Martinez*, 462 F.3d 903 (8th Cir. 2006).

[13] *See, e.g., United States v. Heath*, 259 F.3d 522 (6th Cir. 2001) and *United States v. Rousseau*, 257 F.3d 925 (9th Cir. 2001) and *United States v. Chaney*, 647 F.3d 401 (1st Cir. 2011) and *United States v. Jones*, 700 F.3d 615 (1st Cir. 2012)(specific circumstances "gave rise to a reasonable concern for officer security that justified the use of handcuffs and drawn handguns").

[14] *See United States v. Felix-Felix*, 275 F.3d 627 (7th Cir. 2001); *United States v. Yang*, 286 F.3d 940 (7th Cir. 2002). *See also United States v. Acosta-Colon*, 157 F.3d 9 (1st Cir. 1998)(explaining that handcuffing "does not automatically convert the encounter into a *de facto* arrest" but "when the government seeks to prove that an investigatory detention involving the use of handcuffs did not exceed the limits of a *Terry* stop, it must be

able to point to some specific fact or circumstance" to explain why handcuffing was necessary).

[15] *See Park v. Shiflett*, 250 F.3d 843 (4th Cir. 2001) as an example.

[16] *See, e.g., McConney v. City of Houston*, 863 F.2d 1180 (5th Cir. 1989); *BeVier v. Hucal*, 806 F.2d 123 (7th Cir. 1986)(dicta); and *Thompson v. Olson*, 798 F.2d 552 (1st Cir. 1986)(dicta).

[17] *Miranda v. Arizona*, 384 U.S. 436 (1966).

[18] *Berkemer v. McCarty,* 468 U.S. 420 (1984).

[19] *Oregon v. Mathiason*, 429 U.S. 492 (1977).

[20] *Berkemer v. McCarty*, 468 U.S. 420 (1984).

[21] *Beckwith v. United States*, 425 U.S. 341 (1976).

CHAPTER 3

REASONABLE SUSPICION AND PROBABLE CAUSE

The Fourth Amendment to the United States Constitution requires that all searches and seizures be "reasonable." Searches and seizures are "reasonable" only if there are facts and circumstances that justify them. Unless and until facts and circumstances combine in certain legally sufficient ways, a police officer has no authority to infringe upon anyone's freedom or reasonable privacy expectations.

The factual combinations that justify various searches and seizures have been given names in the law. Some police actions – arrests and full searches, for example – require an amount of factual justification called "probable cause." Certain limited police actions – investigative stops and weapons frisks, as examples – do not require as much factual justification. They are justified by combinations called "reasonable suspicion."

Reasonable suspicion and probable cause are fluid and shifting concepts that depend on the specific facts and circumstances of a situation. Each case is unique. Probable cause and/or reasonable suspicion will crystallize only on the basis of the particular facts of a particular case.

Unless and until facts and circumstances combine in certain legally sufficient ways, a police officer has no authority to infringe upon anyone's freedom or reasonable privacy expectations.

The Definition Of Probable Cause And Reasonable Suspicion

Terminology is important. The terms "reasonable suspicion" and "probable cause" should be used carefully and precisely. The term "probable cause" often is used loosely and mistakenly to describe any lawful basis for an investigative action. That is, when a prosecutor or a judge says that an officer lacked probable cause to stop a vehicle, that person often really means the officer did not "have authority" to stop the vehicle. This loose usage of the term "probable cause" creates confusion and generates problems in criminal prosecutions. An officer can "have authority" to stop a vehicle even when he does not have "probable cause." Many searches and seizures may be justified by a factual basis significantly less than probable cause. Reasonable suspicion will justify many police actions and is much easier to establish.[1] The distinctions between probable cause and reasonable suspicion are significant.

Here are some working definitions:

Probable Cause: Facts and circumstances which, taken together with rational inferences therefrom, would cause a reasonable police officer to **believe**...

a. (To arrest)...that a crime has been committed and that a particular person committed it;

b. (To search)...that evidence of a crime is in the place to be searched;

c. (To seize)...that items are contraband or otherwise evidence of crime, or are lawfully subject to forfeiture to the government under applicable forfeiture laws.

Reasonable Suspicion: Facts and circumstances which, taken together with rational inferences therefrom, would cause a reasonable police officer to **suspect**...

a. (To detain or "stop")...that a person is, has been, or is about to be, involved in criminal activity;

b. (To frisk a person)...that a person subject to lawful detention is armed and constitutes a danger to the officer;

c. (To frisk other areas)...that an area within the immediate control and access of a person lawfully detained contains weapons and that the detainee might use those weapons against the officer;

d. (To conduct a "protective sweep")...that other rooms or spaces in a place where an officer is lawfully present contains would-be assailants who would constitute a threat to the officer.

Establishing Probable Cause And Reasonable Suspicion

Establishing probable cause and reasonable suspicion requires that facts, circumstances, and inferences be articulable.

Establishing probable cause and reasonable suspicion requires that facts, circumstances, and inferences be articulable – explainable in words. Neither probable cause nor reasonable suspicion may be based solely on an unexplainable "hunch" or feeling. In fact, reasonable suspicion is sometimes referred to as "articulable suspicion." In developing inferences, a police officer's training and experience may be, and should be, taken into account. Well-trained and/or experienced officers can detect criminal suspiciousness from circumstances which might be meaningless to untrained and/or inexperienced observers.[2]

Probable cause and reasonable suspicion may be transferred or "imputed." This means that the officer taking an investigative action need not have all operative facts and circumstances in his mind as long as that information is in the mind(s) of others in the chain of investigative action. In fact, if an officer arrests someone on one matter without probable cause, but it turns out that there was probable cause to arrest the person on another matter – of which the arresting officer was originally unaware – the arrest is lawful.[3] The same appears to be true in the case of stops.[4]

Scenario #12 Special Agent Smith works for the Secret Service and has 15 years of experience in investigating crimes involving counterfeit U.S. currency. He is standing in line at a convenience store. When the individual in front of him in line opens his wallet to pay for his purchase, he sees a large number of $50 bills in the man's wallet. S.A. Smith is able to read the serial number on one of the bills and he recognizes the serial number as being inconsistent with how U.S. currency is marked. S.A. Smith approaches the man outside the store, identifies himself as a law enforcement officer and tells the man to stop. The subject submits.

Question: Did S.A. Smith's observation of the serial number give him reasonable suspicion to detain the man?

Answer: Yes. Given his experience in investigating crimes involving counterfeiting, S.A. Smith could articulate why he reasonably suspected that the $50 bill was counterfeit.

Conceptualizing Reasonable Suspicion And Probable Cause

The concepts of probable cause and reasonable suspicion may be viewed as part of a spectrum which could be called a "factual justification continuum." The spectrum might range from "0" (zero) – knowing nothing about a situation – to 100%, being sure or certain of something. It is helpful to look at various factual justifications as they might fall on such a scale.

Absolute certainty is never required in our criminal justice system, even to convict a person of a crime in court. To convict and punish a person for a criminal offense requires "proof beyond a reasonable doubt." If one were to attach a "percentage of certainty" to proof beyond a reasonable doubt, perhaps it might be "98% sure" that a particular person committed a crime.

> **Absolute certainty is never required in our criminal justice system, even to convict a person of a crime in court.**

Below that on a spectrum might be a standard of factual justification called "clear and convincing" evidence. This is the amount of factual justification required in many states to subject a person to involuntary mental commitment, where there must be clear and convincing evidence that a person is a danger to himself or others. This standard would fall above a 50% marker, but below "proof beyond a reasonable doubt."

Just above 50%, but below "clear and convincing," is a standard called "preponderance of the evidence" or the "greater weight of the evidence." It is the standard used in most civil and administrative actions. For the plaintiff to prevail in a civil action, he must prove his case by a preponderance of the evidence. If one were attaching a numerical percentage to that concept, it might be roughly "51% sure" – literally the "greater weight."

The preponderance or greater weight standard was traditionally taught to law enforcement officers as the meaning of probable cause. The concept of probable cause was equated to the phrase "more likely than not," which was often illustrated as "51%" or "the greater weight." Since *Illinois v. Gates,* 462 U.S. 213 (1983), it has become clear that probable cause does not require a showing that something is mathematically probable, or more likely than not. Rather, the probable cause standard requires showing "a fair probability" measured in light of common sense and with benefit of the officer's training and experience.

Thus, probable cause may require (at its lowest levels) something near 50%, but not necessarily 51% or higher. Probable cause can exist even when something is slightly less than mathematically "likely."[5]

Beneath probable cause on the scale is reasonable suspicion, sometimes called "articulable suspicion." Reasonable suspicion is more than unexplainable hunches or feelings, but less than probable cause. Perhaps reasonable suspicion might be shown at "30 - 40% likely" on the scale.

Reasonable suspicion and probable cause do not necessarily require lots of facts. Courts look not only at the number of facts, but the weight of each fact or circumstance, together with inferences and/or deductions that are reasonable in light of the officer's training and experience. Probable cause or reasonable suspicion could come from just one or two facts if they were strong enough. It is not a matter of just counting facts. Instead, it is a matter of looking at all the facts, assessing the importance of each in the totality of circumstances, and making a common sense judgment in light of training and experience.[6] Only then does the officer decide whether there is reasonable suspicion or probable cause. There is no precise formula.[7]

> **Beneath probable cause on the scale is reasonable suspicion, sometimes called "articulable suspicion."**

Sources Of Information

Where and how is information for reasonable suspicion and probable cause gathered? How does one weigh source information for purposes of reaching conclusions? How does one use sources of information to develop reasonable suspicion and probable cause?

Generally speaking, there are two ways one gains information. One is through personal observation or knowledge. That is, we know it ourselves, or we see it, smell it, taste it, or hear it. Firsthand knowledge obviously is normally most useful.[8] If information does not come from personal observation, then it came from somewhere else. This might be a document or another person, for example. For purposes of this chapter, information gained from second-hand sources will be called "hearsay."

Many officers have been led to believe that hearsay cannot be used in a court proceeding. However, for purposes of estab-

> *The use of some types of hearsay information is permitted and normal.*

lishing probable cause and/or reasonable suspicion, the use of some types of hearsay information is permitted and normal.[9]

To assess the reliability of hearsay, one looks mainly at two things:

1. How reliable is the information provider?

2. How does he know the information?

For example, suppose a person reports to police that there is marijuana growing in John Smith's enclosed backyard patio. One first asks whether that information comes from a reliable person, a person who generally should be believed. If the information has come from a reliable person, one still needs to know how the reliable person came by the information. Did he himself see the marijuana growing in that backyard patio or is he reporting something that he has heard from someone else? If a very reliable person tells an officer something, but the reliable person is only passing on what he has heard from an extremely unreliable or unknown source, the information is not necessarily reliable. One must watch for "layers" of hearsay and look for the reliability of information at each level or layer.

> *One must watch for "layers" of hearsay and look for the reliability of information at each level or layer.*

Although they are hearsay, police reports and other official police documents are generally presumed to be reliable because they are usually written in the ordinary course of business by other police officers. However, police documents and reports can and often do include layers of hearsay. Often, reports merely document what someone told another police officer. So, if the report is telling one officer what someone told another police officer, there are two layers of hearsay. If a person telling something to the officer completing the report is merely relating something that the person did not see himself, but heard from someone else, there are three layers of hearsay:

1. The report itself.

2. The person providing information to the reporting officer.

3. The person who provided the original information.

The officer seeking to use the report for purposes of reasonable suspicion and/or probable cause must consider the reliability of the information at each layer. When one presumes that police reports and documents are reliable, one is only presuming that the reporting officer has accurately and truthfully documented what he has been told. That is not necessarily the same thing as believing what he was told.

To establish reasonable suspicion, supporting hearsay information need not be quite so reliable as that required for probable cause. Because reasonable suspicion is a lower standard of evidence than probable cause, it requires less information and demands less in terms of the reliability of the information source.[10] For example, when one is considering "layered" hearsay, the reliability of the information source must be judged more critically when trying to establish probable cause than when trying to develop reasonable suspicion.[11]

Not all hearsay is useful for probable cause or reasonable suspicion. If a drunk person who is also known to be delusional were to approach an officer and tell him that something happened, the officer might not assign the information much weight. To be the basis for probable cause, hearsay must be reasonably reliable.

To be the basis for probable cause, hearsay must be reasonably reliable.

Source Credibility: Why Should This Source Be Believed?

Police Officers

If Police Officer A tells Officer B that A saw something himself, it is reasonable for B to believe it. In the absence of any reason to disbelieve Officer A, if he says he saw it, heard it, tasted it, smelled it, or felt it himself, it is reasonable to believe that Officer A is telling the truth and that it is an accurate report of a personal observation. This issue is long settled.[12] This is why reasonable suspicion and probable cause generally may be transferred, or "imputed," from one officer or police workgroup to another.[13]

> Scenario #13 Police Officer A arrives at the scene of a purse snatching. Police Officer B, who is off duty, tells Police Officer A that he saw John Smith steal the woman's purse.
>
> Question: May Police Officer A arrest John Smith based upon the information he received from Police Officer B?
>
> Answer: Yes. Police Officer A can accept Police Officer B's information as reliable because he is a police officer and he saw the crime occur.

Concerned Citizens

What about other people – just concerned, regular citizens – who state to police that they saw or heard things? May these people be believed for purposes of establishing reasonable suspicion and probable cause? To answer that question, one asks another. Does the source (the ordinary concerned citizen) have any known reason to lie to the police? If the answer to that question is "no," then courts usually presume the information to be reliable.[14]

Again, one must be alert for layers of hearsay. If a concerned citizen source tells police that something occurred, police must ask whether the source was the one who heard, saw, tasted, touched, or smelled it himself – or is he merely reporting what some other person observed? Assuming that the ordinary concerned citizen is reporting a personal observation and has no apparent reason to lie, it is reasonable to believe that the observation is accurate and/or that the statement is likely true. This would be "reasonably reliable" hearsay.[15]

> Scenario #14 A police officer responds to the scene of vandalism to a vehicle. He speaks with the vehicle's owner. The owner found that his tires had been slashed. He tells the officer that a neighborhood troublemaker, John, is the one who slashed his tires. The officer asks the owner how he knows it was John. The owner said that his friend, Mark, heard from Mark's friend, Tony, that John admitted to Tony that he slashed the tires.
>
> Question: Can the officer properly arrest John based solely on the owner's statement?
>
> Answer: No. Although the vehicle owner may be a very honest individual, he has no personal basis of knowledge regarding the accusation he made. The information he is providing is based on multiple layers of hearsay.

Criminal Informants

Criminal informants are a different matter. There is reason to suspect or doubt information that is given by people who are known to be involved in criminal activity. Reasonably reliable information can come from criminals, but more must be done to verify the information – to establish reasons to believe it.[16]

Several factors may make it reasonable to believe information provided by criminal informants. Some criminal informants are paid, which provides at least some incentive to tell the truth. Most such informants realize that if they are not truthful and accurate, they are not likely to continue to be paid for their information.

Another factor is whether the informant has some sort of "track record" – a history of being reliable and providing accurate information.[17] A history or track record of reliability furnishes a basis for believing that the source is reliable. It helps even more if that information has led to arrests, seizures of evidence, and/or convictions in court.

Another way to establish reliability is to verify details of what the informant says. If he tells police that certain facts (X, Y, Z) are true, and if X and Y can be verified as accurate informa-

> *Reasonably reliable information can come from criminals, but more must be done to verify the information.*

tion, it becomes more reasonable to believe that Z is also likely to be true. That sort of verification, checking to see if information is accurate, is called "corroboration." Corroboration can be important and is sometimes required in establishing reasonable suspicion and probable cause. However, if an informant has a sufficient track record of providing accurate information, little or no corroboration may be necessary.[18]

> Scenario #15 John Smith has a lengthy criminal record and no history of providing accurate information to the police. He tells a police officer that stolen merchandise is being stored in a specific house on Main Street. He also tells the officer that a garage on Main Street is selling counterfeit vehicle inspection stickers and that the owner of the garage sells marijuana. A few moments later, another police officer, unaware of the information provided by John, stopped the owner of the garage for a traffic violation and sees marijuana and counterfeit inspection stickers in the car.
>
> Question: Assuming the officer to whom John gave the tip speaks with the other officer about his traffic stop with the garage owner, do they together have enough information to establish probable cause to obtain a search warrant for the house with the stolen merchandise?
>
> Answer: Most likely, yes. The officers were able to corroborate some of the information provided by John – specifically the information concerning the garage owner – making it more likely that the information about the stolen merchandise is also true.

Confidential Informants

Some informants are willing to have their names used in connection with their information and some are not. This is true for both criminal informants and concerned citizen informants. The primary reason that people, ordinary concerned citizens and criminals alike, are unwilling to have their names used is that they fear repercussions and/or retaliation. In some cases, they fear for their safety and their lives. Because police know who the source is, it is often permissible to use such information to establish reasonable suspicion and probable cause even though the source is unwilling to have his name disclosed.

In such a case, however, it is critical to document (and explain in court, if necessary) why the source does not wish to be named. It may also be necessary to provide information confirming that the informant, though unnamed, does in fact exist. If the informant is also a witness to the crime being prosecuted, it may be necessary for the prosecution to either identify the witness or dismiss the case.[19]

> Scenario #16 John Smith witnesses his neighbor smash the window of another neighbor's car, take something and go back to his own residence. John calls the police and identifies the suspect as well as where he lives. The police obtain an arrest warrant and arrest the suspect when he answers the door. The suspect refuses to answer any questions from the police. John wishes to have his identity remain confidential.
>
> Question: During the trial for damaging the vehicle window, will John have to testify?
>
> Answer: Yes. Even though he wishes to remain confidential, John was the only witness to the crime of destruction of property. Alternately, the case may be dismissed.

If the informant is also a witness to the crime being prosecuted, it may be necessary for the prosecution to either identify the witness or dismiss the case.

Anonymous Tips

Because it is unlikely that an anonymous source will have a known track record of reliability, in order to form probable cause from an anonymous tip one would need significant corroboration of certain types of information. Some facts would have to be verified in order to believe that other facts provided were likely to be true. An anonymous tip can provide the starting point, but the amount and type of tip information that can be corroborated will determine whether the tip ultimately leads to reasonable suspicion or probable cause. Anonymous tips that accurately predict future behavior seem to have the best chance of measuring up to legal standards.[20]

Courts have struggled with these concepts. In *Draper v. United States*, 358 U.S. 307 (1959) and *Illinois v. Gates*, 462

An anonymous tip can provide the starting point, but the amount and type of tip information that can be corroborated will determine whether the tip ultimately leads to reasonable suspicion or probable cause.

U.S. 213 (1983), the Supreme Court found that probable cause could be developed through an officer's corroboration of certain neutral details of an anonymous tip regarding criminal activity. Since that is enough, in some circumstances, to establish probable cause, then obviously reasonable suspicion sometimes may be established by a partially-corroborated anonymous tip. However, in *Florida v. J. L.*, 529 U.S. 266 (2000), the Supreme Court held that an anonymous tip that a described person at a described public place was carrying a gun is not, without more, sufficient for reasonable suspicion to stop and frisk, even though corroboration of description, time and place occurred.[21] In *United States v. Long*, 464 F.3d 569 (6th Cir. 2006), a federal appeals court held that a caller who tells police that he is the neighbor of a home then being burglarized is a presumptively reliable citizen informant, not an anonymous source, even though his name was not obtained.

Scenario #17 The police receive an anonymous telephone call saying that Jane Smith, a 24-year old white female with brown hair, will leave her apartment at 123 Main Street, Apt. 4 at 2:30 p.m. this afternoon, get into a red Ford Mustang, and proceed to a motel located at 567 Long Street where she intends to sell the half ounce of cocaine that she will have in her possession when she leaves her apartment. The police proceed directly to the identified apartment and set up surveillance. At 2:35 p.m., they observe a female matching the description of Jane leave Apt. 4 and get into a red Mustang. They follow the car and notice that she is taking the most direct route to the motel mentioned in the tip. The police stop her vehicle as she is pulling into the motel parking lot. During a consent search, they locate a half ounce of cocaine in her purse.

Question: Was the information provided by the anonymous informant sufficient, with this corroboration, to provide the police with reasonable suspicion to stop the car?

Answer: Yes. Though anonymous, the tip contained sufficient predictive information that could be corroborated by the police prior to the stop to establish reasonable suspicion. Therefore the stop was lawful and the consent was not the product of an illegality.

Frequently Recurring Elements Of Probable Cause Or Reasonable Suspicion

Geographical Location Of The Subject

In developing probable cause and/or reasonable suspicion, it is appropriate to consider a person's location. Suppose a person is walking down a sidewalk at night. Walking on a sidewalk is not itself unusual or suspicious. There is no reason to suspect the person of criminal activity based on his location. But suppose a person is hidden in the bushes behind a warehouse. Then the subject's location is appropriately a suspicion factor. If a subject's geographical location is very close to the scene of a recently-committed crime then typically the location factor grows in its significance.

High Crime Area

Suppose the subject is in a neighborhood or an area of town which has been experiencing a very high crime rate. Suppose the subject is on a particular street corner that is very well known for hand-to-hand sales of drugs. Or, suppose the subject is walking down the sidewalk at 3 a.m. in an otherwise deserted neighborhood in which there has recently been a rash of nighttime crime. In all these cases, the subject's location would become a suspicion factor.[22] Although presence in a high crime area is a relevant suspicion factor it will rarely suffice by itself to establish justification for a stop.[23]

> **Although presence in a high crime area is a relevant suspicion factor it will rarely suffice by itself to establish justification for a stop.**

A Caution On The "High Crime Area" Factor

The fact that there have been crimes in the past in a given area does not make that area forever thereafter a high crime area. For an area to be labeled a "high crime area," that label needs to be true in an objective sense – in a way that can be articulated and justified – that there has been some sort of spree or real history of continued crime in this particular area. Statistical comparison to other areas might make the high crime area label more appropriate and significant. It is important that officers not fall into the habit of describing all parts of the community as high crime areas just because there has been some crime in those areas historically.

Time Factor

When is a subject observed? If he is observed very near the place of a crime very soon after a crime has been committed, those two factors combine to assume greater importance. The more time that elapses between when the crime occurs and when a person is observed, the less significant the location factor becomes.

The presence of a person in public, even late at night, is not enough by itself to justify an investigative detention or arrest. With the possible exception of curfews, there is no hour of the night so late that people are generally subject to seizure just for being in public. If a person is walking down a sidewalk at 4:00 a.m., that by itself does not justify an investigative detention. Of course, an officer may approach such a person and attempt to engage him in voluntary contact and conversation. The officer must take care, however, not to allow the contact to escalate into a seizure unless reasonable suspicion or probable cause has developed.

> **The presence of a person in public, even late at night, is not enough by itself to justify an investigative detention or arrest.**

Sensory Perceptions

Obviously, seeing something suspicious should cause suspicion. Hearing suspicious noises should do likewise. An officer's sense of smell can also be extremely important. If, with benefit of training and/or experience, an officer is able to recognize certain odors as suggesting the presence and/or use of illegal drugs, that sensory perception by itself may establish reasonable suspicion or probable cause.[24] Similarly, if during a lawful weapons frisk an officer should touch or feel objects that, though hidden from view, are recognizably a form of contraband (like illegal drugs), the sensory perception may be used for or toward conclusions of reasonable suspicion or probable cause.[25]

Suspect And Criminal Description Similarities

Obviously, if a person closely resembles the description of a person who has committed a crime, there may be reason to believe or suspect that the person might have been the one who committed the crime. How close a fit must there be between the subject's appearance and the reported description? Certainly, a tighter fit is required in order to establish probable cause, while a general similarity can sometimes be sufficient to establish reasonable suspicion.

Just one aspect of a physical description could be enough to justify a seizure of a person if the descriptor is sufficiently rare. If the only thing known about the person who committed a crime ten minutes ago is that he was wearing pink high top tennis shoes with purple stars drawn on them, that in itself would likely provide lawful basis for a seizure of a person who fit this one-factor description, because the factor is so particular and so unusual.

But what if the perpetrator of a summer time, midmorning crime was reported to have been a white male in his mid-twenties wearing blue jeans and a T-shirt? If an officer were to see, a half-mile from the crime scene, an hour after the reported crime, in a densely populated urban setting, a person who fit that description, the description match might be of little significance. However, that same description, at a different time of day, a different location relative to a crime scene, and in an area of lesser population density, might provide the basis for probable cause or reasonable suspicion.

The Suspect's Observed Behaviors

Another important factor is the suspect's behavior before he knows police are present. Is the subject observed, for example, carrying a bag of tools to the back of a warehouse? Is he carrying a gas can to the back of a closed and inactive business late at night? Extreme nervousness and "furtive" gestures also may be considered.

Also significant is a subject's behavior after he sees or is contacted by the police. Again, extreme and unusual nervousness may be considered. Attempts to evade contact with police and certainly out-and-out flight – running in apparent panic at the sight of police – may be considered strong suspicion factors. If an officer were to drive behind a closed and inactive warehouse at two o'clock in the morning and a man standing behind the warehouse were to run when he saw the officer, these facts and circumstances taken together almost certainly form reasonable suspicion that this person is involved in criminal activity.

While running at the sight of police is suspicious, it is not likely, by itself, to establish reasonable suspicion.[26] It is best to assume that at least one additional suspicion factor is required to establish reasonable suspicion, especially in light of *Illinois v. Wardlow*, 528 U.S. 119 (2000), where it took a 5-4 decision of the Supreme Court to find that running at the sight of police, plus presence in an area well known for illegal drug activity, were together enough for reasonable suspicion.[27] Also, a passenger "bolting" from a car stopped for a traffic violation creates reasonable suspicion, according to a federal appeals court in *United States v. Bonner*, 263 F.3d 213 (3d Cir. 2004). The passenger in *Bonner* was initially seized during the traffic stop. By fleeing, the passenger "prevented the police from maintaining oversight and control over the traffic stop," thereby giving the police reasonable suspicion to detain him following a foot pursuit.

Knowledge Of A Subject's Criminal History Or Past Criminal Behavior

What if an officer sees someone walking down the street late at night that the officer knows has a lengthy criminal record of house-breaking and store-breaking offenses? While knowledge of the subject's history and/or criminal record may be taken into account as a suspicion factor, it usually cannot be the exclusive basis for a stop. A person who in the past has been convicted of crime does not lose forever his right to walk freely in public, and may not be stopped solely because he has a record.

But suppose an officer is patrolling a part of town where there has been a recent crime spree involving late-night break-ins. Suppose as well that it is late at night and the officer sees a person the officer knows has a lengthy history of break-in and related offenses. In those circumstances, the subject's record could be strongly considered in the development of reasonable suspicion or probable cause.

Profiling

As an officer gains training and experience, it becomes possible to form reasonable inferences from certain characteristics and behavioral patterns which the trained, experienced officer recognizes as consistent with statistical "profiles" of certain types of criminals and/or criminal behavior. In particular, profiling is often successful in drug enforcement, where some officers possess an enormous backlog of experience and insight which, through training, may be extended to other officers. In *U.S. v. Sokolow*, 490 U.S. 1 (1989), DEA agents relied on a "drug courier profile" that the DEA had developed over time based upon their experiences in combating the drug trade to justify detaining a suspected drug courier at an airport. Some of those "drug courier profile" factors, such as paying $2,100 cash for an airline ticket to a city well known as a destination for drug couriers, staying in that city for a very short period of time before returning home, and travelling under an alias, were present in *Sokolow*. The Court said that "although each of these factors is not, by itself, proof of illegal conduct, and is quite consistent with innocent travel, taken together, they amount to reasonable suspicion that criminal activity was afoot."

It is critical that officers evaluate profile matches in light of all surrounding circumstances and common sense. Profiling should not be done rigidly or mechanically as if it were a simple checklist. The use of race as a factor in profiling is generally inappropriate and usually illegal. Officers must stay closely apprised of both law and policy in this turbulent area, but "profiling," absent illegal discrimination, is not unconstitutional.

> **Profiling, absent illegal discrimination, is not unconstitutional.**

Unusualness

In the past, some case law and a considerable amount of police training suggested that it is "suspicious" if someone is "out of place" or "unusual" in a particular area or neighborhood, particularly during nighttime hours. The conclusion that someone "doesn't belong in" a certain neighborhood also feeds this notion of "suspiciousness." Obviously, one way someone could be judged "unusual" or "out of place" is that his race is inconsistent with neighborhood demographics. Because such judgments, whether reached by "concerned citizens" or by officers, create much potential for racially discriminatory police actions, it is probably wise for police to discount this factor, however "common-sensical" some might feel it to be.

> **The fact that something or someone is unusual in a particular setting is not necessarily criminally suspicious.**

The fact that something or someone is unusual in a particular setting is not necessarily criminally suspicious. People wearing top hats and riding unicycles are unusual but presumably not thereby criminally suspicious. In the desert, both rain and rainbows are unusual – but neither are criminally suspicious. For the "unusual" consequently to be judged suspicious, two more dots must be connected. The particular "unusualness" must also suggest criminal involvement. While some forms of unusualness will satisfy this criterion, a person's skin pigmentation, regardless of neighborhood or hour of the day or night, will not.

Uncooperativeness

What about a person who is very uncooperative when confronted by police? Suppose, for example, that an officer (without reasonable suspicion) walks up to a person and attempts a voluntary contact. The officer says, "Excuse me, sir, do you have a moment I could speak with you?" The subject responds, "No way, I'm in a big hurry. I've got to go."

Suppose the police officer walks along with him (which is permitted) and says, "Sir, where are you going in such a hurry?" Suppose further that the person now gets verbally abusive toward the officer, questioning the officer's motives, saying, "Look, Butthead, why are you harassing me?" The officer replies, "Sir, do you mind if I see some identification?" The man refuses to produce identification, saying, "I'm not showing you any identification. I told you I was in a hurry," and turns to walk away.

In such a situation, lack of cooperation cannot serve as the foundation for reasonable suspicion or probable cause. In general people are normally under no legal obligation to cooperate with police, to answer any questions, or to provide any documentation of their identities.

Even if there is reason to suspect a person of criminal activity and that person is detained, that person generally possesses a constitutionally-guarded right of privacy in respect to the contents of his or her pockets, wallet, or purse. The refusal to relinquish a constitutionally-protected right cannot be used by police as justification for the seizure of a person or for a police-ordered inspection of personal documents. Similarly, a person generally cannot be stopped or arrested for his failure to "explain himself" (i.e., to "justify" his presence in a given place) or even verbal abuse (including profanity and vulgarity) toward the officer.[28]

However, a state or local law that requires, in the context of a lawful investigative detention, that a subject verbally identify himself upon demand of police may be constitutional.[29] Also, if a person is engaged in activities requiring a privilege license (driving, hunting, fishing as examples), an officer may require production of the license, assuming the officer is not inappropriately singling people out for such contacts.[30]

> *The refusal to relinquish a constitutionally-protected right cannot be used by police as justification for the seizure of a person or for a police-ordered inspection of personal documents.*

Officers' Collective Knowledge

Who must have reasonable suspicion or probable cause? Can this be a group activity or must reasonable suspicion or probable cause ultimately be consolidated within the mind of an individual officer? The Supreme Court has not addressed the issue and lower courts are fragmented. Some state appeals courts have held that factual justification must exist, at least based on collective knowledge, within the work group of the officer ultimately taking action.[31] In such an analysis, reasonable suspicion or probable cause could exist even though it has not crystallized in the thoughts of any one officer and even though no one particular officer has the whole fact situation in mind. Other courts have required that the factual justification for an action must have congealed in the mind of at least one officer in the chain of action.

If, however, one officer does have reasonable suspicion or probable cause and he asks or orders another officer to make a stop or arrest, the officer taking the action is factually justified based on the theory of transferred or "imputed" justification. The acting officer does not have to learn all the facts and circumstances which are known to the originating (requesting) officer. If the officer initiating the request or order to arrest has reasonable suspicion or probable cause and another officer acts on that officer's request, the second officer is deemed to have acted with benefit of the first officer's knowledge.

Obviously, for there to be the necessary trust relationship between the officer requesting or demanding and the officer who is taking the action requested or demanded, there must be a basis for that trust. This requires that an officer requesting that another officer take action be certain that the requisite reasonable suspicion or probable cause exists prior to making the request of the other officer.[32]

> Scenario #18 Officer Jones is on routine patrol when he observes a vehicle drive past him, in the opposite direction, travelling over 100 miles per hour. He knows that Officer Davis is patrolling a few miles up the road in the direction that the speeding car was heading. Officer Jones provides a description of the vehicle to Officer Davis. Officer Davis pulls to the side of the road and within a few minutes a vehicle matching the description drives past her but the vehicle is now traveling the speed limit. Officer Davis stops the vehicle.
>
> Question: May Officer Davis lawfully stop the vehicle even though she did not witness any violation of the law?
>
> Answer: The stop was lawful because the information that Officer Jones had regarding the speeding was imputed to Officer Davis. Officer Davis may use information received from another law enforcement officer as the basis for a detention.

NOTES

[1] See, for example, United States v. Sokolow, 490 U.S. 1 (1981).

[2] See, for example, United States v. Cortez, 449 U.S. 411 (1981).

[3] Devenpeck v. Alford, 543 U.S. 146 (2004).

[4] See, for example, United States v. Delfin-Colima, 464 F.3d 392 (3d Cir. 2006).

[5] See Maryland v. Pringle, 540 U.S. 366 (2003), where the Supreme Court stated that the preponderance of the evidence standard "has no place" in a probable cause determination. See also United States v. Romero, 452 F.3d 610 (6th Cir. 2006) and United States v. Chauncey, 420 F.3d 864 (8th Cir. 2005), recent cases applying Pringle.

[6] United States v. Arvizu, 534 U.S. 266 (2002).

[7] Illinois v. Gates, 462 U.S. 213 (1983).

[8] See, for example, United States v. Bishop, 264 F.3d 919 (9th Cir. 2001).

[9] See Draper v. United States, 358 U.S. 307 (1959) and Jones v. United States, 362 U.S. 257 (1960).

[10] See, for example, Alabama v. White, 496 U.S. 325 (1990).

[11] See, for example, United States v. Shaw, 464 F.3d 615 (6th Cir. 2006), where a mother's "bare-bones" allegation to police that her three-year-old son had told her that he had been molested by a particular person created a duty for police to investigate but did not by itself create probable cause to arrest the accused.

[12] United States v. Ventresca, 380 U.S. 102 (1965).

[13] See Whitely v. Warden, Wyoming State Penitentiary, 401 U.S. 560 (1971), United States v. Fiasconaro, 315 F.3d 28 (1st Cir. 2002), and United States v. Sandoval-Venegas, 292 F.3d 1101 (9th Cir. 2002), as examples.

[14] See Guzell v. Hiller, 223 F.3d 518 (7th Cir. 2000).

[15] See United States v. Harris, 403 U.S. 573 (1971) and Kiser v. City of Huron, 219 F.3d 814 (8th Cir. 2000).

[16] *See, for example, United States v. Barnes*, 195 F.3d 1027 (8th Cir. 1999).

[17] *See, for example, United States v. Sidwell*, 440 F.3d 865 (7th Cir. 2006).

[18] *See, e.g. United States v. Riley*, 351 F.3d 1265 (D.C. Cir. 2003).

[19] *See Roviaro v. United States*, 353 U.S. 53 (1957).

[20] *See, for example, Alabama v. White*, 496 U.S. 325 (1990)(anonymous tip plus corroboration enough for reasonable suspicion) and *Illinois v. Gates*, 462 U.S. 213 (1983)(anonymous tip plus corroboration good for probable cause).

[21] *See Alabama v. White*, 496 U.S. 325 (1990), *but compare Florida v. J. L.*, 529 U.S. 266 (2000) for a contrary result in light of differing facts.

[22] *See, e.g., United States v. Arvizu*, 534 U.S. 266 (2002); *United States v. Lindsey*, 482 F.3d 1285 (11th Cir. 2007)(corroborated anonymous tip plus presence in a high crime area) and *United States v. Bumpers*, 705 F.3d 168 (4th Cir. 2013).

[23] *See United States v. Black*, 707 F.3d 531 (4th Cir. 2013).

[24] *See, for example, United States v. Humphries*, 372 F.3d 653 (4th Cir. 2004).

[25] *See Minnesota v. Dickerson*, 508 U.S. 366 (1993).

[26] In *California v. Hodari D.*, 499 U.S. 621 (1991), the Supreme Court approached this issue but did not settle it.

[27] *See also United States v. Mayo*, 361 F.3d 802 (4th Cir. 2004), for a more recent application of this principle.

[28] *See Johnson v. Campbell*, 332 F.3d 199 (3d Cir. 2003).

[29] *Hiibel v. District Court of Nevada*, 542 U.S. 177 (2004).

[30] *See, for example, Delaware v. Prouse*, 440 U.S. 648 (1979).

[31] *See People v. Gomez*, 117 Cal. App. 4th 531 (2004).

[32] *See United States v. Colon*, 250 F.3d 130 (2d Cir. 2001) for an unsuccessful attempt to impute probable cause from a 911 operator to a police officer.

CHAPTER 4

VEHICLE STOPS AND SEARCHES

Though the Supreme Court has explained the law in the area of vehicle stops and searches in more than two dozen cases, considerable confusion still exists in lower courts concerning when a vehicle may be stopped, when it may be searched without a warrant, and exactly what portion of the vehicle may be searched. This chapter will discuss vehicle stops, the various types of warrantless vehicle searches, the justification required to conduct each search, and the scope of lawful search, including whether a closed container in a vehicle may be searched.

Stopping A Vehicle

With narrow exceptions such as certain types of checkpoints, the same factual justification necessary to validate an investigative detention of a pedestrian is required for the stop of a vehicle to detain an occupant. A stop of a pedestrian or vehicle may not be conducted randomly or whimsically; it must be based on reasonable and articulable suspicion of criminal activity. Though probable cause is sometimes required to search a vehicle, it is not required to stop one.[1]

> *A stop of a pedestrian or vehicle may not be conducted randomly or whimsically; it must be based on reasonable and articulable suspicion of criminal activity.*

Scenario #19 A police officer observes a vehicle circling in the parking lot of a closed business at 3:00 am.

Question: May the officer stop the vehicle even if she does not observe a violation of traffic law?

Answer: Yes. The officer has reasonable suspicion that criminal activity may be afoot. This scenario is no different than had the officer seen an individual "casing" a business on foot. In either case, a brief investigative detention to confirm or dispel the officer's suspicion about criminal activity is justified.

Checkpoints

Even stops without any particularized suspicion are lawful under some circumstances. Vehicle "checkpoints," for example, may be permitted in certain regulatory situations, like driver's license and drunk driving checkpoints, truck weigh stations, and border enforcement. However, checkpoints which have as their primary purpose the more general enforcement of the criminal law – like "drug checkpoints" – were outlawed by the Supreme Court in *City of Indianapolis v. Edmond*, 531 U.S. 32 (2000). More recently, the Supreme Court decided that specific information-gathering checkpoints can be lawful and speculated that other checkpoints would be lawful in order to prevent people (terrorists, for example) from entering certain areas and to prevent people (perpetrators) from leaving certain areas.[2] Also, some courts have held that even though most criminal investigative checkpoints are prohibited by *Edmond*, "fake checkpoints" – signage indicating the impending presence of an in fact non-existent checkpoint – may be permitted in order to allow police to scrutinize people's driving behavior upon seeing the signage.[3]

Pretext (Dual Purpose Stops)

"Pretextual stops" are those where the officer's true investigative motives are not reflected in the "objective" basis for the stop. In *Whren v. United States*, 517 U.S. 806 (1996), the United States Supreme Court held that the Fourth Amendment does not prohibit pretextual stops of motor vehicles as long as there is an objectively lawful justification for the stop. For example, the fact that the officer's real motivation for stopping the vehicle was only a "hunch" of drug involvement does not invalidate a traffic stop that is otherwise lawful for, say, an inoperative tail light. An officer's subjective motivation is irrelevant to the Fourth Amendment validity of an objectively lawful, though pretextual, stop. In *Arkansas v. Sullivan*, 532 U.S. 769 (2001), the Supreme Court extended this rule to a pretextual arrest and in *United States v. Petty*, 367 F.3d 1009 (8th Cir. 2004), one federal appeals court extended it to inventory searches.[4]

Also in 1996, the Supreme Court ruled that a pretextual traffic stop does not necessarily have to be ended by the words "you're free to leave now" before an officer moves forward with a request for consent to search. The Fourth Amendment test for a valid consent to search is whether the consent is voluntary,

> **The Fourth Amendment does not prohibit pretextual stops of motor vehicles as long as there is an objectively lawful justification for the stop.**

and voluntariness is a question of fact to be determined from all of the circumstances. The Supreme Court ruled that "it would be unrealistic to require officers to always inform detainees that they are free to go before a consent to search may be deemed voluntary."[5]

> Scenario #20 A police officer observes a car being driven by a man that the officer suspects of being involved in several larcenies over the past few months. The officer has a hunch that the man may have some of the stolen items in his vehicle. He does not have reasonable suspicion. The officer sees the car roll through a stop sign without coming to a complete stop. The officer conducts a traffic stop with the intent in mind to see if he can spot any of the stolen items in the car. The officer is not motivated by the traffic infraction but uses it to get a chance to chat with the driver and make visual observations.
>
> Question: Is this a lawful stop?
>
> Answer: Yes. The subjective intent of the officer is irrelevant so long as there is an objectively lawful basis for the stop, which in this case was the officer's observation of a traffic violation.

Expanding Traffic Stops To Investigate Other Matters

It is not permissible for officers to extend the duration of a stop in order to investigate a matter for which they do not have reasonable suspicion,[6] but officers may ask questions unrelated to the stop and "no reasonable suspicion is required to justify questioning that does not prolong the stop."[7] Several federal appeals courts have approved a short extension of the stop for unrelated questioning, justifying it as a reasonable detention under a "totality of the circumstances" evaluation, or finding that the time spent on unrelated questioning was a "*de minimis*" intrusion. In *United States v. Guijon-Ortiz*, 660 F.3d 757(4th Cir. 2011), an officer calling the Federal Bureau of Immigration and Customs Enforcement (ICE) to ask about the validity of an ID card did not unreasonably prolong a traffic stop because the call to ICE

It is not permissible for officers to extend the duration of a stop in order to investigate a matter for which they do not have reasonable suspicion.

was deemed similar to running a driver's license and registration to check validity. In *United States v. Turvin*, 517 F.3d 1097 (9th Cir. 2008), the Court found that a request for consent to search did not unreasonably prolong the traffic stop when questioning was based on information learned during the stop and minimally extended the duration of the stop. In the case, the officer making the stop learned from another officer that a "rolling methamphetamine laboratory" had been found in the defendant's vehicle earlier that year. The officer paused for only four minutes during the process of writing the traffic ticket, during which time he spoke with the second officer, and then walked to the defendant's vehicle and obtained consent from the defendant to search the vehicle.

Unless officers establish reasonable suspicion to continue the detention, the traffic stop must be ended, and voluntary contact established to pursue the investigation.[8] Officers may not stop a vehicle for something for which there is reasonable suspicion, and then put that matter on the back burner, sliding to the front investigative burner a matter for which there is not reasonable suspicion – all the while continuing a seizure. In *United States v. Macias*, 658 F.3d 509 (5th Cir. 2012), a defendant's "nervousness" was not sufficient to justify extending the stop to unrelated questioning. In *Macias*, a state trooper engaged in detailed questioning about matters unrelated to the defendant's driver's license, his proof of insurance, the vehicle registration, or purpose and itinerary of his trip, with the questioning lasting 11 minutes. In contrast, see *United States v. Bueno*, 703 F.3d 1053 (7th Cir. 2013) for an example of a traffic stop where reasonable suspicion was developed during the course of the stop which made the extension of the stop lawful.

> Scenario #21 A police officer stops a vehicle for running a stop sign in an area where there have been numerous break-ins over the past few weeks, including one the night before. There are no suspects or leads in the break-ins. After obtaining the driver's license and registration, the officer questions the driver for five minutes regarding the break-ins, and asks the driver where he was last night at the time of that break-in. After questioning the driver, the officer returns the license and registration and gives the driver a verbal warning regarding the stop sign violation.
>
> Question: Is this officer's questioning of the driver regarding the break-ins permissible during this traffic stop?
>
> Answer: Probably not. The officer has no reasonable suspicion as to this particular driver's involvement in the break-ins. It is likely that a court will view the extended questioning regarding the break-ins as expanding the scope and duration of the traffic stop.

Actions Related To The Stop

Once a vehicle is stopped, the ordinary rules of arrest, detention, and search apply, including the frisk and plain view doctrines. At the officer's option, occupants may be ordered out of the vehicle for reasons of effectiveness and safety.[9] An officer may enter a lawfully stopped vehicle to search for a Vehicle Identification Number (VIN) even though he has no reason to believe or suspect that the car is stolen, provided the VIN cannot be viewed from outside the vehicle.[10] Such an action to determine a VIN is a reasonable search, though without warrant or probable cause, because:

Once a vehicle is stopped, the ordinary rules of arrest, detention, and search apply, including the frisk and plain view doctrines.

1. The entry is limited in purpose and scope to discovery of a number for which there is no reasonable expectation of privacy;

2. The entry is into an area (a vehicle in a public place) in which expectations of privacy are much diminished; and

3. The governmental interest in regulating vehicles and requiring VINs to be readily visible justifies a limited intrusion to assure the presence of a VIN, and learn what the number is.

> Scenario #22 A police officer stops a car for speeding. While looking through the wind shield, the officer sees that he cannot read the VIN plate that is attached to the top of the dashboard. He orders the driver out of the vehicle so that he can check the VIN on the side of the driver's door. While looking at the VIN on the door, the officer notices a small bag of marijuana lying on the floorboard in plain view.
>
> Question: Is it permissible for this officer to open the car door to check the VIN plate?
>
> Answer: Yes. Therefore, the officer has a lawful basis for the plain view observation.

Consent To Search

This book will deal with the broad principles applicable to consent searches in Chapter 11. The following discussion pertains to how the consent search theory applies in vehicle situations.

In order to be valid, consent to a vehicle search must be obtained from someone who has apparent authority to consent, and the consent must be given voluntarily. The required justification for a consent search of a motor vehicle is voluntary permission from the apparent owner and/or person in control of the vehicle to conduct the search. Normally a person who has possession and control of a rented vehicle that he has borrowed without the rental company's permission would not have a recognized expectation of privacy in that vehicle.[11] However, a vehicle operator may establish a reasonable expectation of privacy in a rented vehicle even if that person's name is not on the rental agreement if it can be established that he had the renter's permission to drive the vehicle.[12] It is not necessary to advise the subject of his right to refuse to consent to the search.

The scope of a consent search is anywhere in the vehicle that could reasonably be thought to be within the scope of the consent. Containers within the vehicle may be searched if it is reasonable to believe that the container is within the bounds of the consent. Doing damage to the area or item to be searched would generally require explicit permission.

In *Florida v. Jimeno,* 500 U.S. 248 (1991), the United States Supreme Court discussed the theory of consent as it related to the search of a container within the vehicle, stating:

> "[The officer] had informed respondent that he believed respondent was carrying narcotics, and that he would be looking for narcotics in his car. We think that it was objectively reasonable for the police to conclude that the general consent to search respondent's car included consent to search containers within that car which might bear drugs."

The *Jimeno* case does not hold that every consent to search a motor vehicle extends to every closed container inside. Rather, the consent to search the car will extend only to those closed containers that it is reasonable to believe were included in the scope of the consent. If the subject is told what the object of the search is and the particular container could be concealing the object of the search, the search is likely lawful given the *Jimeno* decision. For example, in *United States v. Garrido-Santana,* 360 F.3d 565 (6th Cir. 2004), a federal appeals court applying *Jimeno* found that searching a gas tank was permissible, given consent to search "the car."

The person consenting to the search may limit his consent to certain areas of the vehicle and may withdraw his consent at any time.[13] If consent is withheld or withdrawn, no warrantless search may be conducted unless it can be justified by one or another of the exceptions to the search warrant requirement. Refusal to consent or withdrawal of consent may not be used as a factual justification for conclusions of reasonable suspicion and/or probable cause, since a person's refusal to relinquish a constitutional right may not be used as a basis for police action against him.

A person's refusal to relinquish a constitutional right may not be used as a basis for police action against him.

> Scenario #23 A police officer asks the driver of a lawfully stopped vehicle for consent to search her car for drugs. The driver validly consents. When she exits the vehicle, she leaves her purse sitting on the passenger seat. During the search of the car, the officer searches the purse and finds marijuana in the purse.
>
> Question: Was is it lawful for the officer to search the purse?
>
> Answer: Yes. The officer's request to search the car contained no implied limits on the scope of the search and specified that he was looking for drugs. It was reasonable for the officer to believe that since the driver gave her consent and left her purse in the car when she exited, the purse was within the implied scope of this search.

Frisk Of Vehicle For Weapons

Car frisks are lawful on essentially the same basis as would allow the frisk of a person.

Car "frisks" are lawful on essentially the same basis as would allow the frisk of a person. A warrantless weapons frisk of the passenger compartment of a lawfully-stopped vehicle is permissible if the officer has reasonable suspicion that a dangerous weapon is immediately accessible within the passenger compartment. The frisk is limited to places in the interior passenger compartment in which a quickly-accessible weapon could be placed or hidden. Once established, authority to frisk the vehicle remains even though the suspect is removed from the car and held nearby.[14]

A closed container found in the passenger compartment may be opened and checked for weapons if the contents of the container are immediately accessible to vehicle occupants (i.e., the container could be opened quickly without breakage). The trunk usually may not be searched during a frisk of a vehicle for weapons because the contents of the trunk normally are not immediately accessible to vehicle occupants. However, where the trunk is accessible through a rear seat "fold-down," a frisk of the trunk may be permissible.[15]

Scenario #24 A police officer stops a vehicle matching the description (sufficiently for reasonable suspicion) of one involved in an armed robbery 20 minutes ago. The driver, the lone occupant, is removed from the vehicle at gunpoint and handcuffed. The officer then immediately looks under the front seat and in the unlocked glovebox for weapons. From the glovebox, he removes a loaded handgun.

Question: Was the officer's search of the vehicle in this fashion lawful?

Answer: Yes. The officer conducted a vehicle frisk. Given the nature of the crime suspected, he had reasonable suspicion of the presence of a weapon and the scope of the frisk was limited to areas immediately accessible to the occupant.

Scenario #25 A police officer approaches a car that just pulled into a convenience store parking lot because he notices that the driver is a man that he arrested yesterday for unlawfully possessing a firearm that was located in the same vehicle's center console. The officer has no reasonable suspicion that the man is currently engaged in criminal activity and a voluntary contact is made. The driver exits the vehicle and the officer tells the man that for safety reasons he is going to "frisk" the car for weapons. In the center console he locates another firearm.

Question: Was the vehicle frisk in this instance lawful?

Answer: No. The fact that someone was armed in the past does not by itself justify a frisk every time that person is seen by a police officer in the future, or even the next day.

Frisk Of Occupants

The frisk of vehicle occupants is regulated by the general law of frisking – *Terry v. Ohio*, 392 U.S. 1 (1968) and its descendant cases. *Terry* defined a frisk as "a carefully limited search of the outer clothing...to discover weapons..." and indicated that such searches are justified if two conditions are present:

1. Lawful basis for investigative detention; and

2. Reasonable suspicion the suspect is armed and constitutes a potential danger to the officer.

During a traffic stop, reasonable suspicion that a passenger is armed and dangerous justifies a frisk of that passenger without any need for belief that the passenger is otherwise involved in unlawful conduct.[16]

Although a number of state courts, legal scholars, and commentators disagree, it appears that carried articles like handbags and backpacks may be "frisked" upon the same justification as would support a lawful body frisk. Quickly accessible articles and areas within the immediate control of the detainee may be secured and frisked. It does not matter that the item could be moved away from the detainee and thereby secured.[17] In *Michigan v. Long*, 463 U.S. 1032 (1984), the Supreme Court made clear that police are not required to "adopt alternate means to ensure their safety in order to avoid the intrusion involved in a *Terry* encounter."[18]

Scenario #26 A police officer stops a vehicle for speeding. There are four occupants in the vehicle. One of the backseat occupants is known to the officer as a member of a violent street gang. The officer suspects that the subject is armed and dangerous and asks him to step out of the vehicle. She tells him that she is going to pat him down for weapons. She locates a handgun in his waistband.

Question: Was this pat-down lawful?

Answer: Yes. The backseat passenger was an occupant in a lawfully stopped vehicle and the officer's knowledge of his connection to ongoing street gang violence was reasonable suspicion of the presence of a dangerous weapon.

Search Incident To The Arrest Of A Vehicle Occupant

The law controlling vehicle searches incident to the arrest of an occupant was clarified significantly with the Supreme Court's decision in *Arizona v. Gant*, 556 U.S. 332 (2009). Prior to *Gant*, most officers were trained that when an officer lawfully arrests someone from a vehicle, the officer could return to and thoroughly search the passenger compartment as a permissible "search incident to arrest" even if the subject had been secured in a nearby police car. In *Gant*, the Court held that authority for officers to search passenger compartments of vehicles incident to an occupant's arrest is strictly limited to the following two situations:

1. Where the arrestee is unsecured and close to the passenger compartment at the time of the search; and/or

2. Where it is "reasonable to believe" that evidence of the crime of arrest is in the passenger compartment.

Arizona v. Gant clarified *New York v. Belton*, 453 U.S. 454 (1981), which was widely read to mean different, and held that when the arrestee has been removed from the car and secured elsewhere, the officer may not conduct a search of the vehicle incident to that arrest unless the officer has "reason to believe" that evidence of the crime of that arrest will be found in the passenger compartment. In this area of the law, the term "reasonable to believe" as the standard for retrieval of evidence is best viewed as equivalent to reasonable suspicion.

Officers may not *intentionally* leave an arrestee unsecured for the purpose of "manufacturing" a reason to search. If officers deliberately leave the arrestee unrestrained with access to the vehicle in an attempt to justify the vehicle search, courts will likely find the search to be illegal. Searches for evidence related to the crime of arrest are limited to areas where that evidence is likely to be found and will not always include the entire vehicle. For example, a drunk-driving arrest may justify a search for alcoholic beverages or related containers in the passenger compartment but perhaps not in the trunk. The officer's ability to explain why it was reasonable to believe that evidence of the

Searches for evidence related to the crime of arrest are limited to areas where that evidence is likely to be found and will not always include the entire vehicle.

crime of arrest might well be in a certain area will be critical, and training and experience count.

The *Gant* rule does not change the rules regarding a search of the person incident to arrest or departmental inventory requirements, both of which are permitted without any particular reason to believe that evidence is present. Police can also continue to "frisk" the interior of a vehicle for weapons under the *Terry* standard of reasonable suspicion of the presence of a weapon that would constitute a threat.

Scenario #27 A police officer arrests the driver of a vehicle for driving under the influence of alcohol and secures him in a police car. The officer then returns to the driver's car and searches the passenger compartment incident to the arrest, looking for alcohol containers.

Question: Was this vehicle search incident to arrest lawful?

Answer: Yes. The officer had reason to believe that evidence of the crime of arrest (DUI) would be located in the vehicle. Since looking under the driver's seat was reasonably within the scope of this search for evidence, the officer was allowed to look there.

Scenario #28 A police officer arrests the driver of a vehicle on an outstanding warrant for failing to pay child support, then secures him in a nearby police car.

Question: May the officer then search the vehicle incident to the arrest of the driver?

Answer: No. It is not reasonable to believe that evidence of the crime of arrest (failure to pay child support) would be located in the vehicle.

"Carroll" Search (Probable Cause Search)

Many officers have been taught that federal constitutional law requires that, whenever it is practical to do so (i.e., absent an "exigency" or emergency), a search warrant should be obtained before conducting a probable cause vehicle search. In fact, federal constitutional law rarely requires a warrant for a vehicle search. A search warrant is required to search a motor vehicle only when that vehicle is not in a publicly-accessed vehicular area, and then only when exigent circumstances do not justify immediate warrantless action. The Fourth Amendment to the United States Constitution does not require a search warrant for vehicles in public areas and never has, insofar as Supreme Court decisions are concerned.

The Fourth Amendment does not require a search warrant for vehicles in public areas and never has, insofar as Supreme Court decisions are concerned.

An officer who has probable cause to believe that contraband or other evidence of a crime is in an apparently operable motor vehicle that is in a public area may conduct a warrantless search of any part of the vehicle that could contain the object of the search. This includes any closed container, locked or unlocked, that could conceal the item to be seized. Public areas include public streets and roadways and usually include privately-owned properties which are commonly used by the public for vehicular movement (e.g., shopping center and even apartment complex parking lots).

Finding some quantity of illegal drugs in a motor vehicle typically establishes probable cause to believe that more drugs are present. See, for example, *United States v. Rosborough*, 366 F.3d 1145 (10th Cir. 2004), where even a drug dog alert to the passenger compartment allowed a probable cause search of the trunk. See also *United States v. Parada*, 577 F.3d 1275 (10th Cir. 2009), where dog's alert to the front driver's side door gave probable cause to search the entire vehicle and it was not necessary for the dog to indicate the exact source of the odor. But compare *United States v. Jackson*, 415 F.3d 88 (D.C. Cir. 2005), where finding a stolen tag in the passenger compartment plus the driver not having a registration was not probable cause to search the trunk.

Even when police have ample opportunity to obtain a search warrant before searching a vehicle in a public area, the Fourth Amendment does not require a warrant. Though there exists a pervasive myth to the contrary, the Supreme Court has never held that a search warrant is necessary to conduct a probable cause search of a vehicle in a public place. Rather, in a long line of decisions beginning with *Carroll v. United States*, 267 U.S. 132 (1925), the Court has decided consistently that when a motor vehicle is in a public area, it is not subject to the Fourth Amendment's warrant requirement. Motor vehicle privacy rights in public areas are simply not as significant as when the motor vehicle is on private property that is not open to public vehicular access.

> **The Supreme Court has decided consistently that when a motor vehicle is in a public area, it is not subject to the Fourth Amendment's warrant requirement.**

In two 1985 decisions, the Supreme Court reaffirmed its then six-decade-old unwillingness to extend to vehicles in public areas as much Fourth Amendment privacy protection as is accorded homes and other private areas. It also made crystal clear that warrantless searches of vehicles in public areas do not require proof of exigent circumstances. In *California v. Carney*, 471 U.S. 386 (1985), the Supreme Court upheld a warrantless search of a mobile motor home parked in a publicly-accessible parking area and restated that such warrantless searches do not require proof of an emergency or of lack of opportunity to obtain a warrant. According to the Court, such warrantless searches are reasonable, provided they are based upon probable cause, because of either the vehicle's mobility or the reduced expectation of privacy accorded it. Describing what has become known as the "vehicle exception" to the search warrant requirement, the *Carney* Court stated:

> "Besides the element of mobility, less rigorous warrant requirements govern because the expectation of privacy with respect to one's automobile is significantly less than that relating to one's home or office. Even in cases where an automobile was not immediately mobile, the lesser expectation of privacy resulting from its use as a readily mobile vehicle justified application of the vehicular exception."

In the second of its 1985 vehicle search cases, *United States v. Johns*, 469 U.S. 478 (1985), the Supreme Court made its clearest statement regarding exigent circumstances:

> "A vehicle lawfully in police custody may be searched on the basis of probable cause to believe that it contains contraband, and there is no requirement of exigent circumstances to justify a warrantless search."

Today, nearly two dozen decisions of the Supreme Court testify that there is a vehicle exception to the search warrant requirement and that it does not depend on exigent circumstances, lack of time to obtain a warrant, or other impracticalities in obtaining a warrant. The notion that warrantless probable cause searches of vehicles in public areas require special justification beyond probable cause is simply incorrect. A warrantless *Carroll* search may be conducted at the place of the initial contact, or later at a different location. Neither the passage of time nor the relocation of the motor vehicle by officers (even to secure custody) creates a need for a search warrant.[19]

The notion that warrantless probable cause searches of vehicles in public areas require special justification beyond probable cause is simply incorrect.

Two late 1990s Supreme Court decisions re-affirm the continued validity of the now eight-decade-old "*Carroll* Doctrine," *Pennsylvania v. Labron*, 518 U.S. 938 (1996) and *Maryland v. Dyson*, 527 U.S. 465 (1999). Also, in 1999, the Supreme Court held that, in the course of a traffic stop where an officer noticed the driver had a syringe in his pocket and he admitted using it to take illegal drugs, an ensuing warrantless search of a female passenger's wallet-type container was lawful under the *Carroll* Rule.[20]

The notable exception to the *Carroll* Doctrine is if the vehicle to be searched is located on private residential property. Under those circumstances the *Carroll* Doctrine does not apply and rules respecting home and "curtilage" privacy may, and typically would, require a warrant.[21]

> **Scenario #29** A police officer stops a vehicle for a traffic offense. When she walks up to the vehicle, she sees a crack pipe on the seat next to the driver. She orders the driver out of the vehicle, seizes the crack pipe, and searches the rest of the car. In the trunk, she locates a small amount of crack cocaine.
>
> Question: Was the search of the vehicle, including the trunk, lawful?
>
> Answer: Yes. The officer, upon finding contraband (crack pipe), had probable cause to believe there would be more contraband in the vehicle. Under the *Carroll* Doctrine, the scope of the search is anywhere in the vehicle where it is reasonable to expect to find the item being sought.

> **Scenario #30** A police officer responds to a private residence on a call for service. As he is walking up the driveway to the front door, he smells a very strong odor of marijuana coming from the vehicle in the driveway and the officer consequently has probable cause to believe there is marijuana in the vehicle. The officer finds that the car door is unlocked. He opens the door, looks under the seat, and discovers a pound of marijuana.
>
> Question: Was this a lawful vehicle search?
>
> Answer: No. Since the vehicle was on private property, the *Carroll* Doctrine does not apply. The officer needs a search warrant or a valid consent prior to conducting a search, unless an emergency justifies an immediate search, which is not the case here.

Probable Cause Searches Of Containers Within Vehicles

For purposes of this discussion, the term "closed container" refers to any container, open or shut, the contents of which are concealed from view and are not readily apparent. In 1991, the Supreme Court announced that if probable cause to search exists, a closed container found inside a motor vehicle in a public place may be searched without a warrant just as the motor vehicle itself may be. The only requirement for the search is probable cause to believe that evidence or contraband may be inside the container. In *California v. Acevedo*, 500 U.S. 565 (1991), the Supreme Court stated:

> "Until today, this Court has drawn a curious line between the search of an automobile that coincidentally turns up a container and the search of a container that turns up in an automobile. The protections of the Fourth Amendment must not turn on such coincidences. We therefore interpret *Carroll* as providing one rule to govern all automobile searches. The police may search an automobile and the containers within it where they have probable cause to believe contraband or evidence is contained."

The *Carroll* line of cases, including the *Acevedo* decision, creates a simple, easy-to-apply rule. If an officer has probable cause to believe that evidence or contraband is located inside a moveable motor vehicle which is in a public place, a warrantless search for that contraband or evidence is lawful – even if the probable cause information involves a container.

Scenario #31 A police officer stops a car for a traffic violation. When she walks up to the car, she immediately smells the strong odor of marijuana from inside the vehicle. She orders the driver out of the car and begins a search of the car. On the back seat is a backpack.

Question: May the officer search the backpack?

Answer: Yes. If the officer has probable cause to search the vehicle for evidence or contraband, she may also search any closed containers in the vehicle where it would be reasonable to expect to find the object of the search, which would include this backpack.

Inventory Searches

According to the Supreme Court, warrantless inventory searches of impounded motor vehicles serve several important societal interests: They protect the owner's property while it is in police custody; they protect officers against false claims of lost, stolen or damaged property; and they protect the police and community from dangerous instrumentalities. These strong interests make inventory searches reasonable even when there is no reason to believe, or even suspect, that the vehicle contains evidence of a crime, valuables, or hazardous materials.

A warrantless inventory search is permissible if a vehicle has been lawfully impounded and the agency conducting the inventory has a departmental policy requiring inventory searches of all impounded vehicles. Generally, the entire vehicle, including the trunk, if it can be opened without damage, may be searched during the inventory. However, the scope of the inventory search is limited to those parts of the vehicle which are likely locations for important or valuable items or any dangerous instrumentality. Any closed container found may be examined pursuant to a departmental policy if the container is a likely repository for important items or dangerous instrumentalities. The guiding principle regarding scope of inventory is its caretaking purpose; neither the vehicle nor any container should be damaged during an inventory search, unless necessary to deal with dangerous instrumentalities.

> *Generally, the entire vehicle, including the trunk, if it can be opened without damage, may be searched during the inventory.*

If contraband is discovered, probable cause to search for more evidence of that crime and other contraband is created and other vehicle search rules become applicable. Evidence of crime and/or contraband which is discovered during a lawful inventory may be seized and used in a resulting criminal trial.[22]

For an inventory search to be lawful, the impoundment (i.e., police-ordered tow) must be lawful.[23] Not every arrest of a vehicle occupant or discovery of evidence justifies an impoundment of a vehicle. Officers should consult local counsel and state law to determine when vehicles may be lawfully impounded. Also, in *Florida v. White,* 526 U.S. 559 (1999), the Court held that when the vehicle itself is evidence of a crime or is subject to forfeiture, the *Carroll* search warrant exception allows the warrantless seizure of the vehicle.

> Scenario #32 The driver of a vehicle is arrested. The police officer is lawfully impounding the vehicle. The officer has no reason to believe that evidence of the crime of arrest would be in the vehicle. He begins a lawful inventory search of the vehicle and finds that the glove box is locked and no key to it is available.
>
> Question: May the officer break open the glove box in order to inventory its contents?
>
> Answer: No. Since the primary purpose of an inventory search is to protect the property interests of the vehicle owner, intentionally damaging the vehicle or its contents is not allowed.

Summary

In sorting out and applying the various theories of warrantless vehicle search, it is important to keep in mind a basic tenet of the Fourth Amendment – searches must be reasonable. A search is reasonable only when its scope is reasonable, i.e., consistent with its underlying justification. For example, if the justifying theory is suspicion that dangerous weapons might be quickly reached by a suspect, the search may be no more extensive or intrusive than is reasonably necessary to check for weapons which are immediately accessible to the suspect.

A search is reasonable only when its scope is reasonable, i.e., consistent with its underlying justification.

If, during a lawful warrantless search, items which are immediately apparent to be evidence of crime are discovered, those items may be seized then and there under the plain view doctrine of warrantless seizure even if they are unconnected to the evidence and/or crime(s) which were the original justification for the warrantless search.

It is important for officers to understand each theory of warrantless vehicle search and how far each theory can take the officer conducting the search. One type of warrantless search may lead to justification for another type of warrantless search that will permit an even broader, more extensive search.

NOTES

[1] *Delaware v. Prouse*, 440 U.S. 648 (1979).

[2] *Illinois v. Lidster*, 540 U.S. 419 (2004).

[3] *See, e.g. United States v. Martinez*, 358 F.3d 1005 (8th Cir. 2004) and *United States v. Williams*, 359 F.3d 1019 (8th Cir. 2004). *See also United States v. Wright*, 512 F.3d 466 (8th Cir. 2008) for use of a ruse checkpoint to identify which vehicles seek to evade the non-existent checkpoint, and then stopping those vehicles for minor traffic violations.

[4] *See also United States v. Hall*, 497 F.3d 846 (8th Cir. 2007), permitting police discretion in respect to an inventory policy.

[5] *Ohio v. Robinette*, 519 U.S. 33 (1996).

[6] *United States v. Macias*, 658 F.3d 509 (5th Cir. 2011).

[7] *United States v. Mendez*, 476 F.3d 1077 (9th Cir. 2007), *citing Muehler v. Mena*, 544 U.S. 93 (2005) and *United States v. Cochrane*, 702 F.3d 334 (6th Cir. 2012).

[8] *See, for example, United States v. Guerrero-Espinoza*, 462 F.3d 1302 (10th Cir. 2006).

[9] *See Pennsylvania v. Mimms*, 434 U.S. 106 (1977) and *Maryland v. Wilson*, 519 U.S. 408 (1997).

[10] *New York v. Class*, 475 U.S. 106 (1986).

[11] *United States v. Kennedy*, 638 F.3d 159 (3d Cir. 2011).

[12] *See, for example, United States v. Thomas*, 447 F.3d 1191 (9th Cir. 2006).

[13] *See, for example, United States v. Cotton*, 722 F.3d 271. (5th Cir. 2013).

[14] *Michigan v. Long*, 463 U.S. 1032 (1983) is the leading case on frisking a vehicle.

[15] *See, for example, United States v. Arnold*, 388 F.3d 237 (7th Cir. 2004).

[16] *Arizona v. Johnson*, 555 U.S. 323 (2009).

[17] See *United States v. Walker*, 615 F.3d 728 (6th Cir. 2010), upholding the frisk and partial unzipping of a duffel bag to look for weapons.

[18] See also *United States v. Rhind*, 289 F.3d 690 (11th Cir. 2002) and *United States v. Williams*, 962 F.2d 1218 (6th Cir. 1992) for recent incarnations of this principle.

[19] See *Florida v. Meyers*, 466 U.S. 380 (1984) and *Michigan v. Thomas*, 458 U.S. 259 (1982).

[20] See *Wyoming v. Houghton*, 526 U.S. 295 (1999).

[21] See *Coolidge v. New Hampshire*, 403 U.S. 443 (1971).

[22] The Supreme Court decisions which govern this area are *South Dakota v. Opperman*, 428 U.S. 364 (1976) and *Florida v. Wells*, 495 U.S. 1 (1990).

[23] *United States v. Baldenegro-Valdez*, 703 F.3d 1117 (8th Cir. 2013) and *United States v. Arrocha*, 713 F.3d 1159 (8th Cir. 2013).

CHAPTER 5

FORCED ENTRY INTO PRIVATE PREMISES

Privacy rights surrounding private premises, particularly homes, are fundamental under our Constitution. Improper police entries into private premises can cause serious civil liability, massive problems with evidence suppression, and even criminal prosecution of officers. Use of force risks, notably including deadly force, increase dramatically when an officer makes non-consensual entry into a home. Because the risks in this area of policing are so great, this subject should be studied very carefully and be fully understood by every law enforcement officer.

Terminology

The term "forcible" (as used in this discussion) simply means without voluntary consent. "Forced entry" may involve kicking doors, breaking locks, splintering wood, shattering glass, or it may not. A forcible entry is any entry which is made without voluntary consent from someone who has the authority to consent. For purposes of this discussion, "private premises" are residential premises – homes. This term includes rental housing, including hotel and motel rooms. While private offices and other private premises are generally protected by the Fourth Amendment in approximately the same fashion as homes, this discussion will focus on forcible entries by police into homes.

A forcible entry is any entry which is made without voluntary consent from someone who has the authority to consent.

The General Rules For Searches Of Premises

The general rule is that, to force an entry into a home, a warrant is required. An exception to that rule exists in the case of "exigent circumstances." If an officer is forcing entry into a home for the purpose of arresting someone thought to be inside, there are two additional legal requirements, whether or not a warrant is used. First, there must be probable cause to arrest the person believed to be inside. Second, there must be reason to believe that the person to be arrested is actually currently present in the private premises being entered. An arrest warrant does not automatically give the officer the right to enter private premises to look around to see if the person to be arrested is present.

Liability Warning

If an officer is executing an arrest warrant he knows nothing about, it is reasonable for him to assume that the warrant is valid unless there is something on the face of the warrant that clearly indicates it is defective.[1] However, if the officer is aware of the underlying facts and circumstances which give rise to the arrest warrant, and the officer knows those facts and circumstances do not add up to probable cause to believe a crime has been committed by the person subject to the arrest warrant, the officer should not execute that arrest warrant. Instead, the officer should notify prosecutors and/or the court of the issue and seek guidance. The same is true for a search warrant which an officer has reason to believe is invalid.

Reasonable Belief In Arrestee's Presence

Before forcing entry into private premises to arrest, the officer must have a reasonable belief, prior to entry, that the person to be arrested is present at that time in the premises.

Before forcing entry into private premises to arrest, the officer must have a reasonable belief, prior to entry, that the person to be arrested is present at that time in the premises. Though courts differ, most courts use the term "reasonable belief" to mean something less than probable cause,[2] though at least one court has equated "reasonable belief" with probable cause.[3] By using a "reason to believe" standard in *Arizona v. Gant*, 556 U.S. 332 (2009) to justify searching vehicles for evidence of the arrest, the Supreme Court has sparked new debate about the meaning of this standard. Until this matter is resolved by the Supreme Court and given the dire potentials associated with unauthorized entry into private premises, officers are best advised to establish probable cause that the person being sought is physically present in the home prior to forcing entry to arrest.

> Scenario #33 A police officer has an arrest warrant for John Smith. The officer arrives at John's residence and knocks on the door but no one answers. There is a light and a television on inside the residence and a vehicle registered to John is in the driveway. The officer then speaks with a neighbor who says that she saw John go inside the residence 15 minutes ago. He also says that when John's car is in the driveway, he is always home.
>
> Question: May the officer force entry into the residence to look for John?
>
> Answer: Yes. The officer has reason to believe that John is currently home based upon the information the officer has gathered since arriving at John's house.

Exigent Circumstances

There is an exception to the general rule that a warrant is required to enter a home – the presence of exigent circumstances. Exigent circumstances are emergency situations requiring immediate action to prevent imminent danger to life, serious damage to property, the imminent escape of a dangerous criminal, or the destruction of evidence of a serious crime. Over the years, courts have refined the meaning of the term "exigent circumstances" with respect to entering private premises and have made it a stricter and more demanding standard. Some still mistakenly characterize exigent circumstances as any kind of time-critical circumstances. Historically, a common teaching example of "exigent circumstances" might have been "hot pursuit," and there are still appeals courts that characterize all hot pursuits as exigent circumstances. Today, it would seem to be the safer and better view that not every hot pursuit involves exigent circumstances because some hot pursuits might involve extremely minor and non-dangerous subject matter.

The seriousness of the underlying offense or matter is a major factor in determining whether or not there are exigent circumstances.[4] Because the exigent circumstances requirement has become more demanding, and because improper warrantless

Exigent circumstances are emergency situations requiring immediate action to prevent imminent danger to life, serious damage to property, the imminent escape of a dangerous criminal, or the destruction of evidence of a serious crime.

entries into private premises cause such serious risks to officers and to the public, officers should be especially cautious in this area. Danger alone is not sufficient to furnish exigent circumstances; there must be an associated time criticality that makes getting a warrant impractical.[5]

Entry To Arrest

Clearly, officers may enter private premises without a warrant or consent in order to arrest someone in the premises if:

1. Someone is likely to be killed or seriously injured unless immediate warrantless action is taken; or

2. A serious and/or dangerous criminal offender is likely to escape apprehension and/or prosecution unless immediate warrantless action is taken; and

3. There is probable cause to arrest the person sought; and

4. There is reason to believe that the person to be arrested is physically present in the premises at the time of the entry.

Not all crimes or matters are serious enough to present "exigent circumstances." The Supreme Court made clear in *Welsh v. Wisconsin*, 466 U.S. 740 (1984), that the seriousness of the underlying offense is an important factor in determining whether or not there are exigent circumstances. In that case, the Court commented that:

"…It is difficult to conceive of a warrantless home entry that would not be unreasonable when the underlying offense is extremely minor.

"…Application of the exigent circumstances exception in the context of a home entry should rarely be sanctioned when there is probable cause to believe that only a minor offense…has been committed."

In light of the *Welsh* decision, officers are best advised not to force a warrantless entry to arrest unless:

1. The offense is a serious and/or dangerous crime and there is a lack of time to obtain a warrant because the subject is likely to escape or to injure someone; or

2. The arrest process began in a public place and there is an immediate, continuous hot pursuit of the suspect into his home. *United States v. Santana*, 427 U.S. 38 (1976) is authority for the proposition that an arrest that began in a public place or a place exposed to public view – such as the threshold to one's home – cannot be thwarted simply by the arrestee retreating into his home. Officers should be mindful, though, that simply reaching over the threshold into the home constitutes an entry into the home and that entry must either be accompanied by a warrant or a recognized exception to the warrant requirement, like exigent circumstances.[6] Also under the *Santana* rationale, some courts will allow an investigative detention in the threshold of a door opened pursuant to an officer's request.[7] Lower courts are divided on the legality of what some call "warrantless threshold snatchings."

> Scenario #34 A police officer responds to a local convenience store where a shoplifting has just occurred. He views the surveillance footage and sees a man that he immediately recognizes as John Smith take a candy bar from the store without paying. The officer immediately proceeds to John's house. He knocks on the door but no one answers. Through a window, he sees John sitting on the couch. It is obvious that John is not going to come to the door.
>
> Question: May the officer, having probable cause to arrest John, force entry into John's home to arrest him without an arrest warrant?
>
> Answer: No. Given the relatively minor nature of the offense (shoplifting) and the lack of danger to the public associated with the offense, the officer is required to obtain an arrest warrant first. If he returns with an arrest warrant and encounters the same situation, he may then force entry into John's home to arrest him.

Entry To Preserve Evidence

If there is probable cause to believe that critical evidence of a serious and/or dangerous offense is located within private premises and that the evidence is very likely to be destroyed or removed unless immediate warrantless action is taken, the officer may enter without a warrant or consent to secure the premises while awaiting the arrival of a search warrant.[8] Once the premises are secured, no further search should be conducted unless or until:

1. A search warrant for the premises is on scene; or
2. Consent to search has been obtained; or
3. New or additional emergency circumstances arise necessitating additional warrantless search.

There is some risk of evidence loss virtually every time an officer takes the time to obtain a warrant. This does not mean there are always exigent circumstances. To the contrary, only the very likely loss of critical evidence in serious cases will create legally sufficient "exigent circumstances."[9]

> Scenario #35 A police officer on foot patrol in an apartment complex observes through a window in one of the apartments a small bag of marijuana on a coffee table and a young man sitting on a couch.
>
> Question: May the officer force entry into the apartment to seize the marijuana?
>
> Answer: No. There is no emergency here. The officer will need to obtain either a search warrant or the consent of an apartment resident to enter.

Crime Scenes

For purposes of this discussion, a "crime scene" is defined as a location where a crime has very recently occurred or been discovered and where there is an apparent need for investigative action and/or emergency services. Examples include homicide scenes, fire scenes, and scenes of burglaries or break-ins. The mere presence of contraband or evidence in private premises does not make those premises a "crime scene" for purposes of this discussion.

Upon arriving at a crime scene in private premises, officers may enter the premises without a warrant or consent in order to:

1. Locate and secure perpetrators; and/or

2. Provide assistance to injured or others requiring emergency assistance; and/or

3. Locate and secure evidence that is likely to be lost or destroyed by the mere passage of time.[10]

Once exigencies end, consent or a warrant is required. In *Flippo v. West Virginia*, 528 U.S. 11 (1999), the Supreme Court restated that there is no general crime scene exception to the search warrant requirement. Thus, once the actions described in the preceding paragraph are completed, no further search should be conducted unless or until:

1. A search warrant for the premises is on scene; or

2. Consent to search has been obtained; or

3. New or additional emergency circumstances arise necessitating further search.

Scenario #36 A police officer responds to the scene of a residential burglary that just occurred. She is the first officer on the scene and discovers the front door has been kicked open.

Question: May the officer enter the home without a warrant?

Answer: Yes. The officer may enter the home to render aid, secure perpetrators and assure that evidence is not lost to the passage of time. Then, a search warrant or valid consent is necessary for further search activity.

Other Emergencies

Exigent circumstances exist, and officers may enter private premises without a warrant or consent, if it reasonably appears that such action is urgently necessary in order to:

1. Prevent death or serious physical injury; and/or
2. Provide needed emergency medical assistance; and/or
3. Guard against the imminent threat of substantial property damage.[11]

Such actions are "reasonable" under the Fourth Amendment in view of society's interest in police "community caretaking."[12] In *Michigan v. Fisher*, 558 U.S. 45 (2009), the Supreme Court recognized the "emergency aid exception" as one type of exigent circumstance that would permit police to enter a home without a warrant. The emergency aid exception requires an objectively reasonable basis (less than probable cause) for believing that someone needs medical assistance or is in danger.[13] Exigent circumstances also permit a warrantless home entry to prevent immediate harm to persons or property outside of the home. In *Armijo v. Peterson*, 601 F.3d 1065 (10th Cir. 2010), for example, the Court upheld such an entry by the police where the police believed that the occupant of the home was preparing to engage in an imminent act of gang violence at a nearby school. But see also *United States v. Yengel*, 711 F.3d 392 (4th Cir. 2013) for a situation where the Court held that a warrantless search for a grenade inside a home was not justified as an exigency due to the fact that there was no one present in the residence who had access to the grenade.

A federal appeals court, "without recognizing the community caretaking doctrine," says going into a home to get the arrestee a shirt and shoes would not be a sufficient governmental interest to justify a nonconsensual intrusion.[14] But, says a different court, going into a "shot-at" home which was the target of a drive-by shooting was permissible to check human welfare even though there were no signs that anyone was home.[15] Likewise, a 911 hang-up with a no-answer call-back will help justify a warrantless entry under the "emergency aid exception."[16]

> **The emergency aid exception requires an objectively reasonable basis (less than probable cause) for believing that someone needs medical assistance or is in danger.**

> Scenario #37 A police officer responds to a residence to investigate a noise complaint there. Upon arrival, he observes through the front window that there are two people inside physically fighting, assaulting one another.
>
> Question: May the officer force entry into the home?
>
> Answer: Yes. Forced entry may be made in order to prevent serious injury to the two individuals who are fighting.

If A Warrant Is Required, What Kind Of Warrant?

If one does not have an exception to the rule, one is left with the rule – that a warrant is required. If there is no consent, no hot pursuit, and no exigent circumstances, a warrant is required.[17] The question then becomes what kind of warrant? The two usual possibilities are arrest warrant and/or search warrant.

If the police desire to enter a home and there is no consent or exigency present, then a search warrant is usually required. There is a circumstance, however, where an *arrest warrant* alone would provide the authority to enter a home without consent or exigency – if there is probable cause to believe that the home to be entered is the arrestee's residence and that the arrestee is presently there.[18] If the officer wants to enter a home in which the person to be arrested is merely a visitor and not a resident then a search warrant is required. Such homes are sometimes called "third-party premises."

If there is no consent, no hot pursuit, and no exigent circumstances, a warrant is required.

> Scenario #38 A police officer learns that John Smith, on whom there is an outstanding warrant for felony destruction of property, is currently at his grandmother's house at 456 Oak Street. The officer proceeds, with the warrant in hand, to the grandmother's house. The officer knows that John resides at 123 Jackson Street and that is the address listed on the warrant. When the grandmother opens the door, the officer can see John sitting on the couch but the grandmother, after being told about the arrest warrant, will not consent to the officer entering the house.
>
> Question: May the officer force entry into the grandmother's house to arrest John?
>
> Answer: No. Although he has an arrest warrant, the warrant only authorizes the arrest of John, not the intrusion into his grandmother's home to arrest him. The officer will need to obtain a search warrant to enter the grandmother's home if she will not give consent to enter and John doesn't come out voluntarily.

Police-Created Exigencies

The terms "police-created exigencies" and "officer-created exigencies" refer to situations in which police conduct itself creates an exigent circumstance that may then justify their warrantless entry, when prior to their actions there were no exigencies and a warrant or consent would have been required. For example, if the police knock on a door (with or without probable cause), that may prompt people inside to begin disposing of drugs or other evidence and thus "create" exigent circumstances.

Historically, courts were divided on whether to allow this police-generated exigency (imminent destruction of evidence) to justify forced, warrantless entry but most courts were inclined to invalidate these officer-created "exigent" circumstances, especially when the police were intentionally creating the urgency in order to avoid the need to get a warrant. However, in *Kentucky v. King*, 131 S. Ct. 1849 (2011), the Supreme Court reversed this lower court trend and recognized the so-called "police-created exigency" as lawful justification for a warrantless entry, *as long as the police conduct prior to the entry was not itself unconstitutional.* The Court ruled that police are permitted to knock on a door, with or without a warrant, and are not required to seek a warrant as soon as they have probable cause. The Court then offered several acceptable explanations for police deciding to do something other than hurry off to get a warrant. The Court did not determine exactly what the police would have to see or hear from outside a home to establish exigent circumstances, but it made clear that police are permitted to knock on a door and announce their presence, even if their intent is to avoid having to obtain a warrant. It is not permissible, however, for police to engage in conduct that violates the constitution in order to create the exigency, such as, for example, threatening occupants and demanding entry.

Scenario #39 A police officer responds to a residence where he has been told that narcotics are being sold. He intends to do a "knock and talk." He knocks on the door but no one answers. He can see through the window that there are several people inside smoking marijuana. The officer knocks again but this time shouts, "If you don't open this door, I'm going to kick it in!" He then sees the people inside begin to attempt to destroy the marijuana.

Question: May the officer force entry to prevent destruction of the marijuana?

Answer: Probably not. The police officer has impermissibly created the exigency by his actions. Considering that possession of marijuana is a relatively minor offense, the officer is not allowed to force entry to preserve the evidence. Once he threatened to kick the door open, his conduct probably became unconstitutional – though some courts would find that the threat (without action) would not be unconstitutional.

Addresses On Arrest Warrants

Most arrest warrants provide the suspect's residential address, but in many jurisdictions the process by which addresses get put on arrest warrants is not particularly reliable. For this reason, it is best that, in deciding that a particular place is currently the residence of a particular person, officers do not rely exclusively on the address on an arrest warrant and instead confirm that address as being the current residence of the person to be arrested. Obviously, this can be done in a number of ways, some as simple as checking with a neighbor or calling the power company or the phone company to see who currently has service at the address. It would be unreasonable for an officer to force entry into the address provided on the warrant for the purpose of arresting the suspect if the officer knows the address provided is not where the suspect lives. As discussed earlier, there must also be reason to believe that the person to be arrested is present in the home at the time of the warranted entry.

Even if an arrest warrant does not contain the suspect's address, entry into a home may be permissible. For example, in *United States v. Graham*, 553 F.3d 6 (1st Cir. 2009), a police entry into an apartment was upheld as constitutional where the police "reasonably believed" the suspect resided at the apartment, although the apartment address was not on the warrant.

The Knock, Announce And Wait Requirements

Simply having a warrant does not necessarily clear the way for an immediate entry into private premises. In *Wilson v. Arkansas*, 514 U.S. 927 (1995), the Supreme Court ruled that the Fourth Amendment prohibits a "no-knock" forced entry of private premises unless an exigency justifies it. In *Richards v. Wisconsin*, 520 U.S. 385 (1997), the Court clarified *Wilson* and held that notice before forced entry is constitutionally-required unless the officer has at least reasonable suspicion that giving notice would:

1. Endanger someone; or

2. Be futile; or
3. Inhibit effective investigation.

In *Hudson v. Michigan*, 547 U.S. 586 (2006), the Supreme Court held that officers outside a home who could see and hear that a loud physical assault was occurring inside that home were permitted to enter without a warrant, and without knocking and announcing, to attend to the emergency. The officers had reason to believe that knocking and announcing would be futile.[19]

The meaning of "knock" is clear. "Announcing" could mean different things to different people. Normally, if an officer loudly states his or her identity ("Police!") and purpose ("Search Warrant!") the knock and announce requirement has been satisfied. The issue then becomes how long must police wait before making non-consensual entry into the premises. In *United States v. Banks*, 540 U.S. 31 (2003), the Supreme Court held that when executing a search warrant for a comparatively small amount of easily disposed of narcotics, a 15- to 20-second wait after knocking and announcing was sufficient before entering the small apartment where they believed a suspect to be present.

NOTE: State law is frequently more demanding than the Fourth Amendment regarding "no-knock" entries.

Scenario #40 Police arrive at a residence with a narcotics search warrant for the residence. The officers have reliable information that there are weapons in the residence that are quickly accessible by the occupants, who are gang members.

Question: Does the Fourth Amendment require the police to knock and announce their presence and then wait before forcing entry into the residence?

Answer: No. It is reasonable to believe that by knocking, announcing and waiting, the police will be endangering themselves by allowing the occupants an opportunity to arm themselves.

Protective Sweeps

> **A protective sweep is reasonable only to safeguard officers in the pursuit of an otherwise legitimate purpose.**

Protective sweeps involve moving through private premises to determine the presence of would-be assailants and other security threats. "A protective sweep is reasonable only to safeguard officers in the pursuit of an otherwise legitimate purpose."[20] In *Maryland v. Buie*, 494 U.S. 325 (1990), the Supreme Court held that "sweeps," like frisks, may not be performed automatically as "routine officer safety precautions." Instead, also like frisks, a non-consensual sweep requires at least reasonable suspicion of the presence of a threat in the areas to be swept. This suspicion must be articulable and it must be particular.[21] A general concern for officer safety based on a speculative possibility of a threat is not enough.

In *Buie*, however, the Court made clear that if an officer is lawfully present in a room, it is permissible to glance into adjacent spaces for security reasons – even if there is no particularized suspicion.[22] From this it can deduced that the working definition of "protective sweep" is a room-to-room search for security threats – not just taking a quick look into areas adjacent to where the officer is working. A sweep is permitted upon reasonable suspicion of a threat even when the officer is in the home for reasons other than arrest.[23] Where reasonable suspicion of a threat extends to outbuildings or vehicles on the premises, they may be "swept" pursuant to the *Buie* rule.[24]

Scenario #41 A police officer responds to a residence in reference to a domestic assault complaint. The victim tells the officer that her husband hit her, knocking her to the ground in the kitchen. She said that she briefly lost consciousness. She does not know where her husband is.

Question: May the officer perform a protective sweep of the residence without the owner's consent?

Answer: Yes. The officer has reasonable suspicion that a dangerous individual may still be in the residence. For officer and victim safety during the investigation, he may sweep the premises to make sure the husband is not hiding in the home.

NOTES

[1] *Malley v. Briggs*, 475 U.S. 335 (1986).

[2] *United States v. Pruitt*, 458 F.3d 477 (6th Cir. 2006).

[3] See *United States v. Gorman*, 314 F.3d 1105 (9th Cir. 2002).

[4] *Welsh v. Wisconsin*, 466 U.S. 740 (1984).

[5] See, for example, *Fisher v. San Jose*, 509 F.3d 952 (9th Cir. 2007).

[6] See *McClish v. Nugent*, 483 F.3d 1231 (11th Cit. 2007) as an example.

[7] See *United States v. Crapser*, 472 F.3d 1141 (9th Cir. 2007).

[8] See, for example, *United States v. Ruiz-Estrada*, 312 F.3d 398 (8th Cir. 2002).

[9] See *United States v. Rubin*, 474 F.2d 262 (3d Cir. 1973) and consider the *Welsh* decision, discussed above.

[10] See *Mincey v. Arizona*, 437 U.S. 385 (1978); *Michigan v. Tyler*, 436 U.S. 499 (1978).

[11] See, for example, *Brigham City v. Stuart*, 547 U.S. 398 (2006).

[12] See *Cady v. Dombrowski*, 413 U.S. 433 (1973).

[13] See *United States v. Porter*, 594 F.3d 1251 (10th Cir. 2010), applying the "objectively reasonable basis to believe" standard and *Stricker v. Twp. of Cambridge*, 710 F.3d 350 (6th Cir. 2013), applying the emergency aid exception.

[14] *United States v. McGough*, 412 F.3d 1232 (11th Cir. 2005).

[15] *United States v. Huffman*, 461 F.3d 777 (6th Cir. 2006).

[16] *United States v. Elder*, 466 F.3d 1090 (7th Cir. 2006). See also *Johnson v. City of Memphis*, 617 F.3d 864 (6th Cir. 2010) for an example of exigency based on 911 hang-up and other factors.

[17] *Steagald v. United States*, 451 U.S. 204 (1981).

[18] *Payton v. New York*, 445 U.S. 573 (1980).

[19] See also *United States v. Musa*, 401 F.3d 1208 (10th Cir. 2005) for another good example of a permissible no-knock entry. (The

entry and search were for drugs and guns and the suspect had a felony record for violent crimes.)

[20] *United States v. Hassock*, 631 F.3d 79 (2d Cir. 2011)(provides thorough analysis of conflicting circuit court positions related to protective sweeps).

[21] *See, for example, United States v. Moran-Vargas*, 376 F.3d 112 (2d Cir. 2004).

[22] *See United States v. Thomas*, 429 F.3d 282 (D.C. Cir. 2005) for a more recent illustration of this principle.

[23] *See United States v. Miller*, 430 F.3d 93 (2d Cir. 2005) and *United States v. Gould*, 364 F.3d 578 (5th Cir. 2004)(en banc) as examples. For an example of what is enough factual justification for a sweep, *see United States v. Winston*, 444 F.3d 115 (1st Cir. 2006) and *United States v. Cash*, 378 F.3d 745 (8th Cir. 2004).

[24] *See, as examples, United States v. Jones*, 471 F.3d 868 (8th Cir. 2006) and *United States v. Maddox,* 388 F.3d 1356 (10th Cir. 2004).

CHAPTER 6

MIRANDA WARNINGS AND WAIVERS

The Supreme Court's decision in *Miranda v. Arizona*, 384 U.S. 436 (1966) has become part of American culture. The *Miranda* decision is derived from the Fifth Amendment, which in pertinent part prohibits government and government agents from "compelling" someone to incriminate himself in a criminal proceeding. The *Miranda* decision requires that, in certain situations, police inform or advise people of certain rights in order to undo some of the inherent coercion in some such situations. The *Miranda* rule is not offense-specific; it applies the same way to all criminal interrogations, whether they involve felonies or misdemeanors. In *Dickerson v. United States*, 530 U.S. 428 (2000), the Supreme Court held for the first time that the *Miranda* rule is part of the constitutional fabric of the United States and is not merely a technical safeguard. However, in *Chavez v. Martinez*, 538 U.S. 760 (2003), the Court held "mere coercion does not violate the text of the Self-Incrimination Clause absent use of the compelled statements in a criminal case against the witness." The Court then made clear that its decision does "not mean that police torture or other abuse that results in confession is constitutionally permissible as long as the statements are not used at trial."

So, a "mere" *Miranda* violation is unlikely to cause a constitutional rights deprivation unless it is coupled with other serious abuse or unless resulting statements are used at criminal trial against the person whose *Miranda* rights were violated. Intentional *Miranda* violations (to obtain "strategic" advantages) are prohibited even where the subject is subsequently advised of and waives *Miranda* rights. For example, if an investigator chooses to conduct an intentionally illegal ("un-*Mirandized*") custodial interrogation to "get the cat out of the bag" and then takes a "*Mirandized*" version of the same confession, both statements are inadmissible.[1] If the preceding *Miranda* violation is unintentional, a second statement can be saved by the proper use of *Miranda* warning and waiver procedures.[2] And where physical evidence is derived from an illegally "un-*Mirandized*" custodial interrogation, that physical evidence may nonetheless be admissible.[3]

> **Intentional *Miranda* violations (to obtain "strategic" advantages) are prohibited even where the subject is subsequently advised of and waives *Miranda* rights.**

NOTE: While the _Miranda_ Rule itself is a federal law principle, it is possible that a state could create, by statute or interpretation of state constitution, stricter "_Miranda_-type" requirements than exist under Federal law. For example, virtually every state has statutory law governing the interrogation of juveniles. Such laws often include special statutory requirements that go further than the federal _Miranda_ Rule.

The "Custody" Principle

> **The _Miranda_ rule applies only to interrogations which occur in a "custodial" environment.**

The _Miranda_ rule applies only to interrogations which occur in a "custodial" environment. In _Miranda_, the Supreme Court was concerned that the dynamics of custodial police interrogation create an "inherently coercive environment." The Court designed the _Miranda_ rule to help protect a person's Fifth Amendment privilege against compelled self-incrimination in that inherently coercive environment. The heart of the Court's decision in _Miranda_ requires that an in-custody suspect be advised of his rights before police interrogation efforts may proceed. Then, the subject can knowingly decide whether or not he or she wishes to assert or invoke the rights or to waive them. A "waiver" is a voluntary relinquishment or giving up of known rights.

The Supreme Court believed in 1966, and apparently still does, that in the inherently coercive circumstances of police custody, a person could easily forget that he has the right to remain silent and to counsel, and therefore a reminder is necessary. This reminder procedure, what we know today as _Miranda_ warnings, has been called a "prophylactic" rule. It is a protective measure that helps shield the subject from the inherent coercion of custodial interrogation.

A pre-_Miranda_ decision of the Supreme Court, _Escobedo v. Illinois_, 378 U.S. 478 (1964), resulted in what is today a pervasive myth some call "the focus of suspicion" test. This myth has been furthered by lawyers, judges, and law enforcement officers. The myth has it that, when suspicion has focused on a particular person and/or when questioning has become accusatory in nature, that person has become a suspect in a criminal investigation and *Miranda* warnings are therefore required prior to interrogation.

The Supreme Court has squarely rejected the suspect/focus of suspicion test for *Miranda*. In *Beckwith v. United States*, 425 U.S. 341 (1975) and as recently as *Howes v. Fields*, 132 S. Ct. 1181 (2012), the Court announced and clearly settled that "custody, not focus of suspicion," triggers the *Miranda* requirements. *Miranda* applies only when there is both custody and interrogation. So, if there is interrogation but no custody, or custody but no interrogation, the *Miranda* rule does not apply. The rule applies only when a person is in custody and is about to be interrogated by someone he knows to be a police officer. [4]

What Is "Custody"?

Understanding the concept of "custody" is essential to the proper application of the *Miranda* rule. The decision of the Supreme Court in *Berkemer v. McCarty*, 468 U.S. 420 (1984) poses the issue as a question: Would a reasonable person feel he was subjected to those restraints normally associated with formal arrest? Ten years later, the Court re-stated this definition in *Stansbury v. California*, 511 U.S. 318 (1994).

The test for *Miranda* custody is an objective test. In *Florida v. Bostick*, 501 U.S. 429 (1991), though a Fourth Amendment "seizure" case rather than a *Miranda* "custody" decision, the Supreme Court made clear that a "reasonable" person is an innocent person. Presumably, an innocent person does not suffer the anxieties and associated altered perceptions that a guilty person does. Therefore, presumably it does not matter if a guilty person may have felt he was in arrest custody as long as officers did not do or say anything that would cause an innocent person to feel that he was restrained to the degree normally associated with a formal arrest.

In *J.D.B. v. North Carolina*, 131 S. Ct. 2394 (2011), the Supreme Court added consideration of a child's age to the objective "reasonable person" test that determines *Miranda* custody. The Court noted that juveniles generally lack experience and judgment, and are particularly vulnerable to police pressures, so some deference to their youthful perspective is required when determining whether they are in *Miranda* custody.

As discussed in Chapter 2, the Supreme Court recognizes three forms of officer-citizen contact: Voluntary contact, investigative detention, and arrest. *Miranda* "custody" is most easily explained in terms of these three categories. A "voluntary contact" is consensual. The officer has not said or done anything that would cause a reasonable (innocent) person to feel he was being required to participate in the contact. Obviously, voluntary contacts are not custodial and, therefore, in such contacts interrogation is permitted without *Miranda*. Officers who work carefully and artfully through voluntary, non-custodial contact can conduct a large percentage of their interrogations of criminal suspects without *Miranda* warnings or waiver requirements.

> **Voluntary contacts are not custodial and, therefore, in such contacts interrogation is permitted without *Miranda*.**

The second form of officer-citizen contact is the investigative detention or "*Terry* stop." A *Terry* stop is a limited seizure of a person based on reasonable suspicion that the person is, has been, or is about to be, engaged in criminal activity. In two cases, *Berkemer v. McCarty*, 468 U.S. 420 (1984) and *Pennsylvania v. Bruder*, 488 U.S. 9 (1988), the Court has held that *Miranda* warnings are not required for interrogation in a *Terry* stop or investigative detention. The Court reasoned that even though an investigative detention is a seizure under the Fourth Amendment and the subject clearly is not free to leave, it is not the type of custody that the *Miranda* rule was designed to cover. Both *Berkemer v. McCarty* and *Pennsylvania v. Bruder* involved roadside interrogation of a detained motorist, but principles derived from those cases are applicable to other kinds of investigative stops based upon reasonable suspicion. When *Terry* stops become very "arrest-like," *Miranda* custody may exist, as explained below.

The third form of officer-citizen contact – arrest – is generally synonymous with "custody" for purposes of *Miranda*. An arrest is any seizure of a person that goes beyond the limits of a *Terry* stop or investigative detention. While a *Terry* stop is generally a brief, one-location field contact, an arrest typically involves seizures of longer duration or in which persons are required by officers to move involuntarily from one location to another. Involuntary movement of a seized person from one place to

> **An arrest is any seizure of a person that goes beyond the limits of a <u>Terry</u> Stop or investigative detention.**

another is a hallmark characteristic of an arrest in the constitutional sense. Use of force or restraints that are lawfully part of some investigative detentions may nonetheless cause a reasonable person to feel he has been subjected to restraints normally associated with formal arrest. While the term "custody" under *Miranda* has much the same meaning as the Fourth Amendment concept of "arrest," *Miranda* "custody" likely includes the more intrusive *Terry* stops in which force, shows of force, and/or physical restraints are used and continued.[5]

"Custody" for *Miranda* purposes is not necessarily the same as the "custody" associated with arrest. *Miranda* custody can occur prior to an arrest if a suspect is placed in a police-dominated situation where a suspect experiences arrest-like restrictions, and it can occur in an improvised interrogation room within a prison. Applying these principles in *Maryland v. Shatzer*, 559 U.S. 98 (2010), the Supreme Court distinguished between physical custody – Shatzer serving prison time in the general population – and *Miranda* custody, where Shatzer would be removed to a more police-dominated interrogation room for questioning.

> Scenario #42 A police officer responds to the area of a reported armed robbery that has just occurred. He is told that the described suspect pointed a handgun at the victim. Beginning a hunt for the suspect, the officer observes an individual that reasonably matches the description of the suspect walking nearby. The officer approaches the individual, draws and points his service pistol at the individual, orders him to the ground and handcuffs him. He tells the suspect that he is not under arrest but that he is being temporarily detained.
>
> Question: Should the officer advise the suspect of *Miranda* rights before beginning to question him about the armed robbery?
>
> Answer: Yes. Although this encounter is so far only an investigative detention, the officer is using restraints that reasonable people normally associate with being arrested.

Intent To Arrest

The Supreme Court's decision in *Berkemer v. McCarty* is perhaps the most important decision ever rendered regarding *Miranda*. It answers almost all of the most difficult questions concerning custody and the application of the rule. *Berkemer* clearly settles *Miranda* questions concerning situations where probable cause to arrest exists prior to the interrogation or is developed during the interrogation. In either case, the officer's uncommunicated intent to arrest has absolutely no bearing or relevance on the question of *Miranda* custody. If the officer has not said or done anything that would cause a reasonable (innocent) person to believe that he is in arrest-type custody, it does not matter that the officer has abundant probable cause and intends to arrest the individual at the conclusion of the interview. What an officer is subjectively thinking or feeling concerning prospects of arrest are irrelevant, as long as they are not communicated to the subject. This remains true even when the suspect is a juvenile.[6]

> *The officer's uncommunicated intent to arrest has absolutely no bearing or relevance on the question of Miranda custody.*

Scenario #43 A police officer arrives at John Smith's house with an arrest warrant for John for assault and battery. When John answers the door, the officer does not tell John that he has the warrant. He asks to step inside to ask John questions about an assault and battery. John voluntarily agrees and submits to the questioning. After obtaining self-incriminating statements from John, the officer informs him of the warrant and arrests him.

Question: Was the officer required to give John *Miranda* warnings prior to the interrogative questioning?

Answer: No. John was not in custody for purposes of *Miranda* at the time of questioning. Although the officer may have intended to arrest John regardless of whether or not John answered his questions, that fact had not been communicated to John at that point. The officer's uncommunicated intentions do not create "custody."

What Is "Interrogation"?

Even when a suspect is in custody, there is no requirement to give *Miranda* warnings unless the suspect is exposed to police "interrogation." The Supreme Court did not deliver the modern definition of interrogation until the case of *Rhode Island v. Innis*, 446 U.S. 291 (1980), where it held that interrogation is express questioning or its functional equivalent, words or conduct by police that they should know are reasonably likely to elicit an incriminating response from the suspect. Even a single question may constitute "interrogation" and, since words *or conduct* may be interrogation, interrogation can occur without any questions being verbalized.

> *Since words or conduct may be interrogation, interrogation can occur without any questions being verbalized.*

For example, suppose an officer places a suspect in a situation in which an incriminating response is very predictable by confronting him with an item of physical evidence from a crime scene (e.g., a robbery surveillance photograph) that ties him to the crime. This would likely be considered police interrogation even though no questions were verbalized. If the suspect is in custody, such "interrogation" would likely require prior *Miranda* warning and waiver. According to some courts, a two-step tactic of showing or describing evidence to a suspect, then giving *Miranda* warnings, may be permissible.[7]

Miranda applies only to police interrogation. In the case of *Illinois v. Perkins*, 496 U.S. 292 (1990), the Supreme Court held that, if an in-custody suspect does not know his questioner is a police officer, there is no "inherent coercion" potential and *Miranda* does not apply. The reasoning of the Court was that a person cannot be coerced by police interrogation if he does not know his questioner is a police officer. *Illinois v. Perkins* involved the insertion of an undercover police officer into a jail facility to attempt to elicit incriminating information from a jail prisoner in regard to a crime with which he had not yet been formally charged. Had the undercover officer attempted to ask questions about a crime for which the prisoner had already been formally charged, then a violation of the Sixth Amendment right to counsel would have occurred.

NOTE: The Sixth Amendment right to counsel provides additional legal protection to a person who has been formally charged with a crime. In that case, police are prohibited from deliberately eliciting incriminating evidence in regard to the formally charged offense, unless a valid waiver of Sixth Amendment rights has first been obtained.[8]

> Scenario #44 John Smith is arrested for larceny. While John is sitting in the back of a patrol car, an officer says, "I don't want you to answer me. I just want to tell you something. The victim just wants his stuff back. If you would just tell us where the stuff is and allows us to return it to him, I'm sure he will drop the charges." John responds with self-incriminating statements.
>
> Question: Would this conversation between the officers be considered "interrogation" for purposes of the *Miranda* rule?
>
> Answer: More than likely, yes. This conversation would probably be considered to be one that police should know would elicit an incriminating response from John, despite the comment, "I don't want you to answer me."

The *Miranda* Warning

There is no magical written or verbal recipe for *Miranda* warnings. Rather, the *Miranda* rule simply requires that the following "message" be conveyed to anyone who is about to be subjected to custodial police interrogation:

1. You have the right to remain silent;

2. Anything you say can and will be used against you in court;

3. You have the right to talk with a lawyer and to have a lawyer with you during any questioning;

4. If you want a lawyer and cannot afford one, one will be appointed to represent you at no cost to you.

There is not an exact set of words that must be read verbatim in order to convey the Miranda *message.*

This is one version of a *Miranda* warning. All versions must convey these messages or they will be deemed insufficient. However, there is not an exact set of words that must be read verbatim in order to convey the *Miranda* message. In *Florida v. Powell*, 559 U.S. 50 (2010), the Supreme Court upheld a

Miranda advisement form that failed to specifically inform the suspect that the right to counsel applied during questioning. The Court found that when read in its totality, the form sufficiently informed the suspect of the *Miranda* rights. The Supreme Court only requires that the *Miranda* message be conveyed in an understandable way.[9] See *United States v. Murphy*, 703 F.3d 182 (2d Cir. 2012) for an example of a case where an officer's "incorrect formulation" of the *Miranda* warning was so poorly worded that it negated the subsequent waiver of rights given by the suspect.

The Supreme Court ruled in *Colorado v. Spring*, 479 U.S. 564 (1987) that an officer does not have to inform a person of "all possible topics" or of the nature of the investigation as part of an advice of *Miranda* rights. However, it is not advisable for an officer to deceive the suspect concerning the subject matter of the pending custodial interrogation. While courts generally allow certain kinds of deception by police during interrogation, provided the suspect is mentally competent, the type of deception that must always be avoided is that which could affect the voluntariness of a waiver of rights. For example, a suspect who believed he was being questioned on a misdemeanor matter might waive his rights when, had he known the questioning actually concerned a murder, he instead might have chosen to remain silent and/or to seek legal counsel. However, in *United States v. Whitfield*, 695 F.3d 288 (4th Cir. 2012), the Court found that such a tactic was lawful in this particular case after a careful consideration of the totality of the circumstances surrounding the interrogation.

Re-warnings

If an interrogation is interrupted, questions may arise as to when and if *Miranda* "re-warnings" are necessary to resume questioning. The Supreme Court has not addressed this issue, but lower courts have set out factors to consider in deciding whether a "re-warning" of *Miranda* rights is necessary following a break in an interrogation:

1. The time span since the last *Miranda* warning;
2. Is the same or a different location being utilized for the interrogation?

3. Is the same or a different officer conducting the interrogation?

4. Are there apparent changes in the suspect's mental or emotional state?

5. Is the same or different subject matter being discussed?

The threshold issue regarding re-warnings is whether the suspect is still aware that his earlier understood *Miranda* rights are still in effect. Even a 20-hour break in an interrogation may not require a re-warning if all other factors relative to the interrogation remain the same.[10] No one factor will necessarily be conclusive. The greater the uncertainty, the greater the need for a *Miranda* re-warning (and possibly re-waiver).

> *The threshold issue regarding re-warnings is whether the suspect is still aware that his earlier understood **Miranda** rights are still in effect.*

Scenario #45 John Smith is arrested for robbery by the State Police. He is brought to State Police headquarters and is questioned by a State Police investigator. John waives his *Miranda* rights and answers questions concerning the robbery charge. After the interrogation, the State Police learn that the FBI wants to speak with him regarding a homicide in another state. An FBI agent arrives eight hours later to interrogate John.

Question: Should the FBI agent re-advise John of his *Miranda* rights and obtain another waiver before beginning the interrogation?

Answer: Yes. It has been eight hours since the last waiver, the questioning concerns another crime altogether, and a different law enforcement official is conducting the interrogation.

The *Miranda* Waiver

A *Miranda* warning by itself is legally insignificant. A valid *Miranda* waiver, however, is of great legal consequence. The significance, then, of giving a *Miranda* warning is that it puts the officer in a position to obtain a valid waiver of those rights. A waiver in this context is a voluntary relinquishment of a known right. What the *Miranda* warning does is to establish this known set of rights.

A typical waiver question is: "Having these rights in mind, are you willing to answer questions now without a lawyer present?" An affirmative response generally shows a voluntary relinquishment of known rights assuming, of course, that no unlawful coercion occurs during this process. A waiver of *Miranda* rights does not have to be in writing or even explicit. Any clear expression of willingness to have questioning proceed without a lawyer present may show a waiver.[11]

> Any clear expression of willingness to have questioning proceed without a lawyer present may show a waiver.

In *Berghuis v. Thompkins*, 560 U.S. 3710 (2010), the Supreme Court held that, after assuring that a subject understands his rights (and assuming he has not invoked them), police *may begin* questioning without first obtaining an explicit or implied waiver. It is still necessary for police to establish that the subject waived the *Miranda* rights before the subject's statement will be admissible in court, but the waiver may be implied from the subject's conduct *during* the questioning. Answering questions, nodding, and participating in the conversation can establish an implied waiver. It is now clearly permissible to proceed with questioning without a prior waiver as long as there is clear indication that the subject understands his rights. If the subject answers questions without a lawyer present, knowing that he does not have to, he demonstrates that he is willing to do so and has implicitly waived his rights.

Scenario #46 John Smith has been arrested and is now being interrogated by a police officer about the crime for which he was arrested. After giving John a *Miranda* warning, the officer asks John if he understands his rights. John says, "yes" and there is no reason to think otherwise. The officer begins asking John questions about the crime and John begins providing incriminating answers.

Question: Has John validly waived his *Miranda* rights?

Answer: Yes. John has implicitly waived his rights by answering the officer's questions without a lawyer present when he just said that he knows he is not required to do so.

Exceptions To The *Miranda* Requirement

There are generally two situations in which an in-custody suspect may be questioned without *Miranda* warnings and waiver. The first is the "public safety exception" to the *Miranda* rule. In the case of *New York v. Quarles*, 467 U.S. 649 (1984), the Supreme Court made clear that when there is an objectively reasonable need for an officer to protect himself or the public from immediate danger associated with weapons, prompt questioning of the suspect regarding the location of the weapon(s) may occur without a *Miranda* warning and waiver.[12]

Standard booking questions may be asked of an in-custody suspect without the need for Miranda warnings and waiver.

Also, standard booking questions may be asked of an in-custody suspect without the need for *Miranda* warnings and waiver, although it is possible to obtain incriminating information from such questions (e.g. nicknames, aliases, home addresses for a subsequent search, etc.). Booking questions are not within the *Miranda* rule because they are not the type of questions that the *Miranda* decision was designed to cover.[13] Booking-type questions may be permitted without *Miranda* even if the booking process is not underway.[14]

> Scenario #47 A police officer is in foot pursuit of a man who just bought drugs from an undercover officer. The man runs inside a crowded grocery store and is eventually caught and arrested in the store by the officer. While searching the man, the officer discovers an empty gun holster on the man's belt. The officer, concerned that there is a gun somewhere in the store, asks the man what he did with the gun. The man says that he dropped it in one of the aisles.
>
> Question: Should the officer have given *Miranda* warnings before asking incriminating questions about the gun?
>
> Answer: No. Even though the man was in custody for purposes of *Miranda*, the officer's question involved an immediate and serious public safety risk.

Volunteered Statements

"Volunteered" statements are not exactly the same thing as "voluntary statements." To be admissible and trustworthy, all statements, including those resulting from interrogation, must be "voluntary" in the sense that they are not "compelled" by government coercion. Volunteered statements, on the other hand, which are sometimes called "spontaneous utterances," are words or statements from a subject that are not prompted by interrogation. Only custodial interrogation requires a *Miranda* warning and waiver. If a subject is volunteering information without interrogative stimuli, *Miranda* is simply not applicable. The resulting statements are admissible in evidence whether or not *Miranda* warnings were given and a waiver was obtained.

The *Miranda* decision itself makes this point clear. In the event that a subject begins volunteering information, officers may simply listen carefully and are not required to interrupt. Short clarifying questions concerning a volunteered statement also may be permissible without *Miranda* warnings or waiver. For example, suppose an in-custody armed robbery suspect spontaneously asks his arresting/transporting officer, "Have you guys found the gun yet?" The officer responds, "What gun are you talking about?" The suspect replies, "You know, my gun, the one from the robbery."[15]

NOTE: This exchange is from a real case.

If a subject is volunteering information without interrogative stimuli, Miranda is simply not applicable.

NOTES

[1] *Missouri v. Seibert*, 542 U.S. 600 (2004).

[2] *Oregon v. Elstad*, 470 U.S. 298 (1985). See also *United States v. Fellers*, 397 F.3d 1090 (8th Cir. 2005).

[3] See *United States v. Patane*, 542 U.S. 630 (2004) and *United States v .Gonzalez-Garcia*, 708 F.3d 682 (5th Cir. 2013).

[4] See *Illinois v. Perkins*, 496 U.S. 292 (1990).

[5] See, as examples, *United States v. Martinez*, 462 F.3d 903 (8th Cir. 2006) and *United States v. Newton*, 369 F.3d 659 (2d Cir. 2004), both involving a handcuffed detainee.

[6] *Yarborough v. Alverado*, 541 U.S. 652 (2004).

[7] See, as examples, *United States v. Gonzalez-Lauzan*, 437 F.3d 1128 (11th Cir. 2006) and *Hairston v. United States*, 905 A.2d 765 (D.C. App. 2006).

[8] See *United States v. Henry*, 447 U.S. 264 (1980).

[9] *California v. Prysock*, 453 U.S. 355 (1981).

[10] See *United States v. Gell-Iren*, 146 F.3d 827 (10th Cir. 1998) for a modern discussion of this issue, and *United States v. Pruden*, 398 F.3d 241 (3d Cir. 2005) where a 20-hour break in the interrogation did not necessitate a *Miranda* re-warning because all other factors had remained constant (the Court noted this was a "close case").

[11] *North Carolina v. Butler*, 441 U.S. 369 (1979). See also *Burket v. Angelone*, 208 F.3d 172 (4th Cir. 2000) as an example.

[12] See *United States v. Reyes*, 353 F.3d 148 (2d Cir. 2003) and *United States v. Ferguson*, 702 F.3d 89 (2d Cir. 2012).

[13] See *Pennsylvania v. Muniz*, 496 U.S. 582 (1990). See also *Rosa v. McCray*, 396 F.3d 210 (2d Cir. 2005), where the suspect was asked his "real hair color."

[14] See, for example, *United States v. Gaston*, 357 F.3d 77 (D.C. Cir. 2004).

[15] See *United States v. Rhodes*, 779 F.2d 1019 (4th Cir. 1985) and *United States v. Cordova*, 990 F.2d 1035 (8th Cir. 1993) as other examples.

CHAPTER 7

THE RIGHT TO COUNSEL AND THE RIGHT TO REMAIN SILENT

Patrol officers and investigators often want to use, as evidence in criminal trials, statements which were made by the defendant and are incriminating in nature. Whatever the degree to which a defendant's prior statements are incriminating, it is likely that the prosecutor's efforts to use the statements at trial will be met with defense objections, often in the form of pretrial motions to suppress the evidence. When these defense objections and/or motions are argued, often at pretrial suppression hearings, the defense attorney will try to show that the incriminating statements were obtained illegally. If the prosecution cannot prove the contrary, the statement generally may not be used at trial, because of the "exclusionary rule." A statement that is suppressed under the exclusionary rule may not be used to prove the prosecution's case, but in some circumstances it may be used to impeach the suspect if he gives contrary testimony in his defense.[1] The same constitutional rights violations may result in police civil liability as well.

Evidence and liability problems regarding a suspect's incriminating statements usually fall into one or more of four categories – each involving a claim that the defendant's constitutional rights were violated. They are:

> *Evidence and liability problems regarding a suspect's incriminating statements usually fall into one or more of four categories – each involving a claim that the defendant's constitutional rights were violated.*

1. The statement was the product of an unlawful Fourth Amendment seizure of the defendant's person – an arrest without probable cause or investigative detention without reasonable suspicion (as earlier discussed).

2. The interrogation did not comply with the *Miranda* rule (as earlier discussed) and/or the associated protections of the rights to silence and counsel, if asserted.

3. The statement was obtained in violation of the defendant's Sixth Amendment right to counsel.

4. The statement was a product of unlawful coercion in violation of the Fifth Amendment protection against compelled self-incrimination and the Fourteenth Amendment requirement that, to be admissible, an incriminating statement must be voluntary.

Although these four claims involve interrelated legal theories, each represents a separate, independent constitutional issue. Each represents a liability threat to police as well as the obvious threat to evidence admissibility.

The first two of these claims have been discussed in Chapters 2 and 6. This chapter focuses on the issues raised by the third and fourth of the claims:

1. Whether or not police may attempt interrogation after a person attempts to assert a right; and

2. What procedure must be followed to obtain a valid waiver of a right, if a waiver is required?

Right To Counsel Issues

The right to counsel comes in two varieties. One is the right to counsel created by the Supreme Court in the *Miranda* decision. This *Miranda*-based right to counsel is associated with the Fifth Amendment right to remain silent and is designed to help protect a person subject to in-custody interrogation from being compelled to incriminate himself. This *Miranda*-based Fifth Amendment right to counsel, famously familiar as the *Miranda* warning "you have a right to an attorney," is separate and distinct from the right to counsel created specifically in the language of the Sixth Amendment.

The differences between the two rights to counsel are important. The Fifth Amendment or *Miranda* right to counsel is present any time there is police interrogation of a person who is in arrest-type custody. The Sixth Amendment right to counsel only arises or "attaches" when formal charges have been brought and protects the defendant from any "deliberate elicitation" of self-incriminating information. The Sixth Amendment right to counsel protects the defendant even in many non-custodial settings and may impose different waiver requirements. Also, rules regarding interrogation after assertion of rights vary according to which right has been asserted.

What Rights Have "Attached"?

Some constitutional rights apply only in certain limited circumstances. A person does not always "own" every constitutional right. For example, a person does not own the Sixth Amendment right to counsel unless and until he is formally charged in a criminal proceeding. When a constitutional right has become applicable in a certain situation, that right has "attached." The significance of attachment is twofold:

1. Once a right has attached, a valid waiver of that right must occur before any interrogation – or, in the case of the Sixth Amendment right to counsel, "deliberate elicitation" – takes place; and

2. Once a right has attached, a suspect may assert that right and thereby impose special additional restrictions on further interrogation efforts by police. It is critical to understand when various rights attach.

> **When a constitutional right has become applicable in a certain situation, that right has "attached."**

When The Right To Silence Attaches

The right to silence is a function of the Fifth Amendment privilege against compelled self-incrimination, which holds that no person shall be compelled to be a witness against himself in a criminal case. This right exists during every police interrogation, both custodial and non-custodial but, in *Miranda v. Arizona*, the Supreme Court required police to *inform* suspects of this "right to remain silent" only prior to conducting custodial interrogations. Still, the right applies at all times.

Scenario #48 A police officer responds to an assault and battery complaint. The victim tells the officer that John Smith just assaulted him. The officer locates John nearby and, without arresting or even detaining him, simply begins asking him questions about the assault. John says he wants a lawyer. The officer ignores John's request and continues asking him questions.

Question: Is the officer required to cease questioning when John says he wants a lawyer?

> Answer: No. Although the officer is interrogating John, John is not in "custody" for *Miranda* purposes and *Miranda*-based rights have not attached.

When The <u>Miranda</u>-Based Fifth Amendment Right To Counsel Attaches

The Fifth Amendment right to counsel was created by the Supreme Court as part of the *Miranda* rule. Because it is a *Miranda* right, it attaches only when a person is in arrest-type custody and is to be interrogated by police. A waiver of this right is therefore unnecessary unless those two conditions (custody and interrogation) occur simultaneously. Arrest alone does not trigger this protection, nor does non-custodial interrogation.

When The Sixth Amendment Right To Counsel Attaches

The Sixth Amendment right to counsel attaches only when someone is "formally charged" with a crime.

The Sixth Amendment right to counsel attaches only when someone is "formally charged" with a crime. Formal charging occurs when someone is indicted by grand jury or is "arraigned." Arraignment is a formal, in-court notification to a defendant that he is charged with a particular crime. In many states, this court appearance is commonly referred to by other names, like "preliminary hearing" or "first appearance." Whatever name it goes by, formal charging is generally characterized by the involvement of a prosecutor who brings the charge(s) formally against the defendant, thus marking the commitment of the government to prosecute. Merely taking an arrestee to a magistrate or similar judicial official for jailing or bonding generally is not formal charging, even though the arrestee may be informed by a judicial official of the charges against the arrestee.

What Words Constitute The Assertions Of Rights By Suspects?

It is critical that officers listen carefully to the exact words of a suspect as he asserts or speaks of asserting rights. Only unambiguous and unequivocal assertions constitute valid assertions of rights. Ambiguous, equivocal "assertions" of rights are not binding on police.[2] Ambiguous statements resembling assertions of rights may be clarified by questions or discussion concerning the suspect's wishes. Notes and/or recordings should be kept documenting the suspect's exact words, whenever possible.

If a suspect says, "I don't want to talk about this anymore," the right to silence has been asserted. A statement, "I'm not sure I want to talk about this, I may need a lawyer," is ambiguous and equivocal and therefore does not validly assert the right to counsel. The cases in the area sometimes draw very fine lines. "Can I have a lawyer?" was an unambiguous assertion, said the Seventh Circuit Court of Appeals in *United States v. Lee*, 413 F.3d 622 (7th Cir. 2005), as was "Can you call my attorney?"[3] Contrast this with *United States v. Shabaz*, 579 F.3d 815 (7th Cir. 2009), where the same Court ruled that a suspect's question "Am I going to get a lawyer?" did not assert his right to counsel. Officers may wish to resolve ambiguity in the suspect's intentions by attempts to clarify, but federal law does not mandate such efforts.

> Scenario #49 A police officer is interrogating John Smith after arresting him. After being given *Miranda* warnings, John acknowledges that he understands his rights, then says to the officer, "I wonder if I should have a lawyer for this."
>
> Question: Is the officer required to ask John if he is invoking his right to counsel with his statement or may the officer simply proceed with efforts to question?
>
> Answer: No. Federal law does not require that the officer attempt to clarify John's wishes. He has stated that he understood his rights. The officer may continue with the interrogation until John clearly, unambiguously and unequivocally asserts the right to silence and/or to counsel.

If An Attached Right Has Been Asserted, What Then?

If an attached right has been asserted, then three questions must be answered:

1. When, if at all, may police later attempt to obtain a waiver and proceed with interrogation efforts?

2. If further interrogation efforts are lawful, what crimes may police bring up for discussion?

3. What, exactly, is necessary for a valid waiver of any rights which have attached?

Assertions Of The Right To Silence

If an in-custody suspect asserts to would-be interrogators the right to silence, that right must be "scrupulously honored." This means, at a minimum, that police must at least temporarily stop their interrogation efforts. In *Michigan v. Mosley*, 423 U.S. 96 (1975), which involved an in-custody assertion of the right to silence, the Supreme Court permitted a resumption of police interrogation efforts after Mosley's assertion was "scrupulously honored" for several hours.[4] It may have helped police that, when they resumed their questioning, it was in respect to a different crime.

Scenario #50 John Smith clearly invokes his right to remain silent in a custodial interrogation. The police officer then asks John, "Are you sure you want to do that? You could really help yourself out by talking to me." John is drawn back into the dialogue.

Question: Are the officer's statements to John after his assertion of his right to remain silent permissible?

Answer: No. Once John has invoked his right to remain silent in the face of custodial interrogation, the officer must immediately and scrupulously honor that request. The officer's statements here are an effort to continue questioning (and may be otherwise coercive).

Assertions Of The Sixth Amendment Right To Counsel

The Sixth Amendment right to counsel prohibits police from deliberately eliciting incriminating information from a criminal defendant *in any matter in which he has been formally charged*, unless he has validly waived that right.[5] "Deliberate elicitation" obviously includes interrogation but can have much broader meaning and is largely self-defining.

In *Montejo v. Louisiana*, 556 U.S. 778 (2009), the Supreme Court discussed law enforcement's authority to interrogate a formally-charged suspect where the suspect has not asserted the right to counsel. The Court in *Montejo* allowed police to approach a formally-charged defendant to attempt to deliberately elicit incriminating information from him regarding the formally-charged offense, as long as: 1) The defendant had not asserted the right to counsel directly to or in the presence of police, and 2) police first obtained a waiver of the Sixth Amendment right to counsel. *Montejo* reiterates that a standard *Miranda* warning and waiver procedure will suffice to produce a valid waiver of the Sixth Amendment right to counsel as well, whether or not the defendant is already represented by counsel. The *Montejo* rule applies where there has been no assertion of the Sixth Amendment right to counsel or when that right has been asserted in court, but *does not apply* when the right has been asserted directly to or in the presence of police at or after formal charging. This reversed a stricter rule that had been in place since 1986. So, officers no longer need to determine whether the defendant invoked his right to counsel in a preliminary hearing at which police were not present because, even if he did, he may still be approached and may still waive his right to counsel pursuant to a proper *Miranda* advisement and waiver process. Also, as was always true, if a defendant himself initiates discussion of an offense with police, whether it has been formally charged or not, police may then proceed with efforts at deliberate elicitation, including interrogation. If the defendant reasserts the right to counsel, the police effort must stop.

Montejo does not change the rule of *Edwards v. Arizona*, 451 U.S. 477 (1981), which deals with assertion of the separate and distinct *Miranda*-based right to counsel (created by the Supreme Court in *Miranda v. Arizona* to safeguard the Fifth Amendment protection against compelled self-incrimination) in the context of custodial interrogation. The *Miranda*-based right to counsel protects a suspect in any custodial interrogation, whether or not

Montejo reiterates that a standard _Miranda_ warning and waiver procedure will suffice to produce a valid waiver of the Sixth Amendment right to counsel.

he has been formally charged with the matter to be discussed. A defendant has the Sixth Amendment right to counsel only in those matters in which he has been formally charged.

> Scenario #51 John Smith has been formally charged (in court) with aggravated assault and there he asked that the Court appoint him a lawyer. He is being held in jail without bond. A police officer, acting undercover as an inmate in the jail, asks John questions about the formally-charged assault. John makes incriminating statements to the undercover officer.
>
> Question: Has the officer violated John's Sixth Amendment right to counsel?
>
> Answer: Yes. This right attached when John was arraigned and it protects him from law enforcement efforts to deliberately elicit incriminating statements regarding the formally-charged offense without a prior waiver of the Sixth Amendment right to counsel.

Assertions Of The Miranda-Based Fifth Amendment Right To Counsel

Once an in-custody suspect asserts the *Miranda*-based right to counsel in a *Miranda* environment (i.e. when exposed to custodial interrogation efforts by police), police are prohibited from all further interrogation efforts on all crimes unless the suspect initiates the communication concerning his criminal involvement, or counsel has been made available to the suspect and counsel is present,[6] or a prison resident has experienced a "14-day break" in *Miranda* custody.[7] Even police who are unaware of the earlier assertion of rights are prohibited from re-initiating interrogation efforts; the burden is on law enforcement to learn of the earlier assertion of rights.[8]

The burden is on law enforcement to learn of the earlier assertion of rights.

In *Maryland v. Shatzer*, 559 U.S. 98 (2010), the Supreme Court created the 14-day break in the *Miranda* custody rule that now permits police to re-initiate efforts to interrogate a suspect living in prison who previously asserted the right to counsel during custodial interrogation, but only after the suspect has been free from *Miranda* custody for at least 14 days. Specifically, *Shatzer* holds that returning a prison inmate to the general prison population for a period of 14 days (after police investigators had him in a prison interrogation room where he invoked his right to counsel) satisfies this rule. The Court reasoned that the general prison population is the subject's familiar environment where he has some degree of control over his situation, more so than he has in a police dominated interrogation room – so it is akin to "going home." It is unlikely, however, that returning a pre-trial detainee to a jail cell for 14 days would satisfy this rule because a pre-trial detainee's presence in a jail facility would unlikely be deemed his "familiar environment."

Though experts persistently debate the issue, *Shatzer* probably does not prevent police from approaching and questioning *sooner than 14 days* a former pre-trial detainee who asserts the *Miranda*-based right to counsel and then leaves custody altogether.[9] *Shatzer* is not clear on this issue, but it appears a pre-trial detainee who invokes the right to counsel in a *Miranda* environment and then leaves *Miranda* custody may be approached by police without regard to the 14-day rule, because the defendant is not in custody at all at that time and *Miranda* protections simply do not apply. A more conservative view is that *Shatzer's* "14-day rule" prohibits police from re-initiating interrogation of a former pre-trial detainee (who has earlier asserted the *Miranda*-based right to counsel) for 14 days after he has left *Miranda* (jail) custody. Time will tell which of these two views is correct.

Scenario #52 John Smith is arrested for robbery and Detective A is preparing to interview him. *Miranda* warnings are given and John invokes his right to counsel. Detective A naturally stops the interrogation effort and John returns to his jail cell. A few hours later, Detective B, who wants to speak with John about his involvement in an unrelated homicide, visits John at the jail. Detective B, from another jurisdiction, is unaware that John has asserted his right to counsel to Detective A. Detective B advises John of *Miranda* rights. John agrees to speak with Detective B about the homicide, and he confesses to it during that interview.

> Question: Will John's confession regarding the homicide be admissible in trial?
>
> Answer: No. While in *Miranda* custody, John invoked his right to counsel to Detective A. That blocks all further police-initiated interrogation efforts on all matters, by all investigators, from all jurisdictions, as long as John remains in pre-trial detention.

Initiation Of Case Discussion By The Suspect

In all of the above-stated rules, the prohibition is of *police-initiated* efforts to interrogate or otherwise deliberately elicit incriminating information from a suspect who has earlier asserted his rights. If the suspect himself or herself initiates with police new discussion of his or her involvement in the crime at issue, the door is opened for police to resume their efforts at questioning. Depending on circumstances, it may be the case that new warning and waiver procedures are required prior to resumption of such efforts.

> Scenario #53 John, under arrest for burglary, invokes his right to counsel following *Miranda* warnings by a police officer. The officer leaves the room. Ten minutes later, the officer returns to transport John to booking. John says to the officer, "I changed my mind. I want to tell you what happened." John has not yet spoken with a lawyer.
>
> Question: May the officer now resume interrogation efforts?
>
> Answer: Yes. John has initiated the new discussion of the case; therefore, the officer is allowed to resume efforts at questioning. Ideally, John would be re-advised of his *Miranda* rights and give a waiver of rights before interrogation proceeds.

What Constitutes A Valid Waiver Of Each Right To Counsel?

The question of what constitutes a valid waiver of *Miranda* rights, the rights to silence and to counsel in custodial interrogations, has been fairly well settled for some time. Officers are familiar with *Miranda* warning and waiver procedures and they are the subject of countless cards, forms, and other writings. Until 1988, however, the Supreme Court had not furnished any significant guidance regarding the requirements for a valid waiver of the Sixth Amendment right to counsel. Lower courts had been divided on the subject, but the Supreme Court's decision in *Patterson v. Illinois*, 487 U.S. 285 (1988) cleared the air, holding that a standard *Miranda*-style waiver procedure is sufficient to produce a valid waiver of the Sixth Amendment right to counsel, at least if the suspect is also advised that he has been formally charged with the specific crime that police wish to discuss. In *Montejo v. Louisiana*, 556 U.S. 778 (2010), the Supreme Court clarified that even if a suspect asserts his right to counsel at an arraignment, is appointed counsel, or is otherwise represented by counsel, police may still approach the suspect for the purpose of attempting interrogation as long as the right to counsel has not been asserted directly to, or in the presence of, police. Through the standard *Miranda* advisement and waiver protocol, the suspect has an opportunity to clearly assert the right to counsel. An unambiguous assertion of the right to counsel requires the police to cease questioning and refrain from further interrogation efforts.

When a person who is not in custody and has not been formally charged voluntarily chooses to talk with police about a matter under investigation, he need not be advised of his rights and a waiver of his rights is implied from his choice to remain with police and talk to them.

> *Through the standard Miranda advisement and waiver protocol, the suspect has an opportunity to clearly assert the right to counsel.*

> Scenario #54 John Smith is arrested for embezzlement. At his arraignment, he tells the Court he wants a lawyer. Police are not present, except for court personnel, and John has not earlier asserted any rights to police. The next day, a police officer visits John at the jail in an effort to discuss the formally-charged offense. The officer tells John that the officer would like to discuss the embezzlement and gives John a standard *Miranda* warning. John explicitly waives his rights and confesses.
>
> Question: Has the officer violated John's Sixth Amendment right to counsel, the right that John invoked at his arraignment?
>
> Answer: No. An assertion of the Sixth Amendment right to counsel is only binding on police if it is made in their presence. Otherwise, an attempt to get a waiver of rights is permissible.

Summary

The suspect's rights, and rules concerning them, may come and go as conditions change during investigation and prosecution.

The law regarding attachment, waiver, and assertion of interrogation rights is evolving, growing, and sometimes confusing. More than one right may be in play at any given time. The suspect's rights, and rules concerning them, may come and go as conditions change during investigation and prosecution. Without close attention to these developments, the criminal investigator is almost certain to make dangerous constitutional errors in the interrogation process. The best way to avoid such errors is to consider each of the three possible rights individually and systematically, one by one, in light of the factual situation in a particular case, at a particular time.

In aid of this process, what follows is a re-statement of the constitutional rules for police dealing with assertions of various interrogation rights, followed by a chart that may help as well.

Assertion Of Right To Silence By In-Custody Suspect

• Examples of valid assertions of this right: "I do not want to talk to you." "I don't want to answer any more of your questions."

- Cease all interrogation efforts immediately.
- No further interrogation efforts on anything until:
    - The suspect has been left alone by police for at least several hours, or
    - The suspect initiates new discussion with police of his involvement in criminal activity, or
    - The suspect leaves custody.
- If further in-custody interrogation becomes lawful, a waiver of rights, using standard *Miranda* warning and waiver procedures, will still be necessary for suspects who remain in custody. If the suspect is no longer in custody, there is no requirement of a *Miranda* warning and waiver. The suspect's choice to meet and talk with police will show his waiver.

NOTE: When a suspect who is not in custody chooses to meet with and talk to police, it is clear that he is not asserting his right to remain silent. Therefore, if during non-custodial interrogation a suspect asserts his right to remain silent, police may continue to attempt questioning. The suspect is free to not respond and free to leave, if he wishes. His decision to remain and to respond to further questions indicates his choice to speak with police rather than to assert his right to silence. When an in-custody suspect asserts the right to silence, the assertion must be scrupulously honored.

When a suspect who is not in custody chooses to meet with and talk to police, it is clear that he is not asserting his right to remain silent.

Assertion Of <u>Miranda</u>-Based Fifth Amendment Right To Counsel By In-Custody Suspect

- Examples of valid assertions of this right: "I am not going to talk to you without my lawyer." "I want to talk to a lawyer first." "I think I want a lawyer."
- Cease all interrogation efforts immediately.
- No further interrogation efforts on anything until:
    - Counsel is actually present at any subsequent interrogation, or
    - The suspect initiates new discussion with police of his involvement in criminal activity, or
    - The suspect is no longer in custody, or

• A prison resident experiences a break in *Miranda* custody by leaving an interrogation environment and returning to the general population for at least 14 days.

If further in-custody interrogation becomes lawful, a waiver of rights, using standard *Miranda* warning and waiver procedures, will still be necessary. (If the suspect is no longer in custody, this right is no longer applicable and no waiver of it is necessary.)

NOTE: This protection is a creation of the <u>Miranda</u> Rule and applies only when <u>Miranda</u> applies. <u>Miranda</u> rights do not attach unless a person in arrest-type custody is exposed to police interrogation; therefore, they may not be validly asserted in non-custodial interrogation. In a non-custodial interrogation, if the suspect would prefer to consult with a lawyer rather than continue talking to police, the suspect has the option of leaving and going to see a lawyer. The Sixth Amendment right to counsel, if attached, may be validly asserted by persons who are not in custody.

Assertion Of Sixth Amendment Right To Counsel Directly To, Or In The Presence Of, Police By Formally Charged Suspect

• Examples of valid assertions of this right: "I want a lawyer." "I would like to have a lawyer appointed for me."

• Cease interrogation regarding the formally-charged crime immediately.

• No further interrogation efforts regarding the formally-charged crime until:

• Counsel is actually present at any subsequent interrogation, or

• The suspect initiates new discussion with police regarding the formally-charged crime.

• If further interrogation becomes lawful, a waiver will still be necessary. A waiver may be obtained by advising the suspect that he has been formally charged with a particular named offense, that police wish to discuss the formally-charged matter, then using standard *Miranda* warning and waiver procedures.

NOTE: This right has nothing to do with custody or non-custody. The Sixth Amendment right to counsel applies only to matters in which a suspect has been formally charged. Assertion of this right blocks further interrogation efforts only on the formally-charged offense. Police may still approach the suspect in an effort to discuss uncharged crimes. (Warning: Sometimes a suspect will assert other rights which may protect him from all interrogation efforts during a period of custody.)

A Final Note – "Voluntariness" And Coerced Statements

To be admissible in evidence, an incriminating statement must not only clear the above-discussed hurdles, it must be made "voluntarily" and not be "compelled" by unlawful government coercion.[10] Determination of what is unlawful coercion and when a statement is voluntary tends to involve the interplay of three factors: (1) The conduct of the government agent (interrogator); (2) the susceptibilities of the subject (confessor); and (3) the environment in which the activity (interrogation) occurs.

Some coercions are so extreme and obvious that virtually any resulting statement would be judged involuntary. Physical abuse and/or deprivation, threats and/or promises in exchange for confession, and other extreme forms of will-bending are all likely to fall into this category.[11] But consider comparatively innocuous statements like "You'll feel better if you get this off your chest – that's a promise." In fact, within a certain spectrum of government behavior there is a sliding scale of acceptability that depends substantially on the two other factors.

For example, deceptive interrogative tactics like pretending to have evidence which, in fact, does not exist may well be permitted if the suspect is intelligent, criminally experienced, and "used to" playing such games.[12] Used on an inexperienced, mentally challenged juvenile, such deception would almost certainly be impermissible. The susceptibilities of the individual suspect to a particular form of coercion will often decide whether that coercion is legally acceptable. Other "susceptibilities" could include cognitive impairments stemming from drunkenness,

> **Some coercions are so extreme and obvious that virtually any resulting statement would be judged involuntary.**

drugs, heavy medication, pain, and the like. "Tricks that are likely to induce a false confession render that confession inadmissible because of its unreliability, even if it is otherwise voluntarily obtained."[13]

Similarly, the environment of the interaction will significantly influence whether certain levels and types of coercion will be permitted on certain types of suspects. Perhaps the most coercive environment is police custody – because any coercion is inescapable. In fact, the Supreme Court's reason for creating the *Miranda* rule was the "inherently coercive" effect of police custody. As a single factor, of course, custody does not render a derivative statement involuntary.

In any event, determining "voluntariness" involves a few absolutes and many variables. Telling someone that, if he confesses, he will receive a lighter sentence or no imprisonment is too much. Telling someone "I don't make the deals, the prosecutor does. If you cooperate, I'll make sure the prosecutor knows it" is usually permitted. Like many other areas of police law, legal determinations of voluntariness are heavily fact dependent.[14]

> Scenario #55 John Smith is being interrogated by a police officer regarding John's arrest for larceny. During the interrogation, the officer says to John, "Look, if you go ahead and cooperate with me now, I will make sure you get probation on this thing and you won't have to go to prison." John then confesses.
>
> Question: Is this confession going to be admissible in trial?
>
> Answer: No. This is an example of an illegally coerced confession.

WHAT RIGHTS ARE THERE?	WHEN DOES RIGHT EXIST? ("ATTACH")	WHAT IS A SUFFICIENT WAIVER?	IF AN ATTACHED RIGHT IS UNAMBIGUOUSLY ASSERTED TO POLICE, WHAT THEN?
"Right to Silence" This is the Fifth Amendment-based right not to be compelled by government to be a witness against oneself in a criminal proceeding.	This right exists all the time unless granted immunity from criminal prosecution or consequent use of resulting statement in a criminal prosecution.	Miranda warnings, acknowledgment of understanding of rights, plus clear indication of willingness to answer questions. (Waiver may be explicit or implied, see text).	No further police-initiated interrogation on anything for at least a few hours. After that, the subject may be re-approached to see if he would be willing to consider further questioning. No badgering.
Miranda-Based ("Fifth Amendment") Right to counsel. Note: This right is not found in the Fifth Amendment but was invented by the United States Supreme Court in Miranda v. Arizona in 1966 to support the new rule.	This right exists when Miranda is in play, i.e., custodial interrogation. But in a non-custodial interrogation effort, it would be asserted by leaving rather than remaining and answering questions.	Miranda warnings, acknowledgment of understanding of rights, plus clear indication of willingness to answer questions without a lawyer present. (Waiver may be explicit or implied, see text).	No further police-initiated interrogation efforts on anything, by any investigator from any jurisdiction, whether or not they are aware of the assertion, unless counsel is present or the subject leaves custody (14-day rule, see text).
Sixth Amendment Right to Counsel	This right exists at and after formal charging (indictment or arraignment) but applies only to the formally-charged offense and not to other matters, even if factually related.	Standard Miranda warning and waiver procedures will suffice, according to the Court, though this is not a Miranda-based right and it applies even in non-custodial settings.	No further police-initiated interrogation efforts regarding the formally-charged offense unless counsel is present. Discussion of non-charged matters may be okay if not blocked by other rules above.

NOTES

[1] *Kansas v. Ventris*, 556 U.S. 586 (2009).

[2] See *Davis v. United States*, 512 U.S. 452 (1994) and *Paulino v. Castro*, 371 F.3d 1083 (9th Cir. 2004)(applying *Davis*) for right to counsel and *Berghuis v. Thompkins*, 130 S. Ct. 2250 (2010) for right to remain silent.

[3] *United States v. Hunter*, 708 F.3d 938 (7th Cir. 2013).

[4] *Michigan v. Mosley*, 423 U.S. 96 (1975).

[5] See *Fellers v. United States*, 540 U.S. 519 (2004).

[6] See *Minnick v. Mississippi*, 498 U.S. 146 (1990).

[7] See *Maryland v. Shatzer*, 559 U.S. 98 (2010).

[8] See *Arizona v. Roberson*, 486 U.S. 146 (1988).

[9] See *Bobby v. Dixon*, 132 S. Ct. 26 (2011), which reminds that *Miranda* and *Miranda*-related protections simply do not apply if a defendant is not in custody.

[10] *Schneckloth v. Bustamonte*, 412 U.S. 218 (1973) and *Arizona v. Fulminante*, 499 U.S. 279 (1991).

[11] See, for example, *United States v. Lopez*, 437 F.3d 1059 (10th Cir. 2006).

[12] *Frazier v. Cupp*, 394 U.S. 731 (1969).

[13] *Aleman v. Village of Hanover Park,* 662 F.3d 897 (7th Cir. 2011)(officer told a suspect that three doctors had all said that a baby's death was caused by being shaken, when no doctor had said any such thing – suspect responded that if that's what the doctors said it must be true).

[14] See, for example, *McCalvin v. Yukins*, 444 F.3d 713 (6th Cir. 2006).

CHAPTER 8

SEARCHES OF PERSONS

Searches of persons involve substantial risks, physical and legal, to the law enforcement officer. They also involve some of America's most valued freedoms. The following discussion will address the following constitutional issues: (1) When and if a frisk search is permitted; (2) the permitted extent and limit of a lawful frisk search; (3) when and if a search incident to arrest or probable cause search is permitted; (4) the permitted extent and limit of a search incident to arrest; and (5) inventory search rules and procedures.

Frisk Searches

The landmark case dealing with frisk searches is the Supreme Court's decision in *Terry v. Ohio*, 392 U.S. 1 (1968). In *Terry*, the Court defined an officer's authority to conduct a limited search of a person for weapons during some investigative detentions, or "stops." For a weapons "frisk" to be reasonable, and thus constitutional under the Fourth Amendment, the preceding seizure of the subject's person (the stop) generally must be lawful and there must be an objectively reasonable basis for the frisk itself.

A frisk is a limited search of outer clothing and sometimes carried belongings for weapons. The main purpose and justifying theory of a frisk search is officer protection. The Supreme Court has characterized the frisk as a "search" because it constitutes an intrusion upon a person's reasonable privacy expectations. The Court has recognized that it is sometimes reasonable for an officer to conduct a protective search for weapons even when the officer does not have probable cause to arrest.

Just as an investigative stop must be supported by articulable circumstances that establish reasonable suspicion of criminal activity, a frisk must be supported by an articulable reasonable suspicion that a lawfully stopped person is armed and constitutes a threat to the officer. As is true also for stops, reasonable suspicion to conduct a frisk may be based on the officer's own knowledge and personal observations or from reasonably reliable information supplied by others, plus reasonable inferences which training and experience allow. Information from anonymous sources is not considered reliable without additional indicators of

The Court has recognized that it is sometimes reasonable for an officer to conduct a protective search for weapons even when the officer does not have probable cause to arrest.

credibility. In *Florida v. J. L.*, 529 U.S. 266 (2000), the Supreme Court held that an anonymous tip that a particular person at a particular place is carrying a gun is not, without more, sufficient for reasonable suspicion to stop and frisk.

During a traffic stop, a passenger may be frisked for weapons based on reasonable suspicion that the passenger is armed and dangerous. No additional belief that the passenger is involved in criminal conduct is necessary to justify the frisk for weapons.[1]

> Scenario #56 A police officer responds to a call of a suspicious individual walking up the street peering into the windows of parked cars. Upon arrival, the officer sees an individual matching the description of the suspect. He approaches and stops the suspect and tells him that he is going to pat him down "for officer safety" though he has no particular reason to think the subject is armed.
>
> Question: Is the frisk in this instance lawful?
>
> Answer: No. Although this is probably a lawful investigative detention, the officer does not have reasonable suspicion that the suspect is armed. A pat-down is not automatically justified in every investigative detention.

> Scenario #57 A police officer sees a man walking down the street that he knows to be a convicted felon and therefore barred from possessing a firearm. The last two times this officer has encountered the man, he has been armed with a firearm. The officer approaches the man, stops him and immediately pats him down.
>
> Question: Is this frisk lawful?
>
> Answer: No. The pre-requisite for a lawful frisk is a lawful stop. A person cannot be stopped and frisked just because he's been criminally involved in the past.

Suspicion Factors For Frisk Searches

The justification for an investigative stop is not necessarily also justification for a frisk. In each case, an officer conducting a frisk must be prepared to point to the specific, articulable facts that justified that particular frisk. Possible factors in the justification for a frisk search include:

Specific Information

Information received from witnesses or other sources may suggest that a person is armed. Even anonymous source information may be considered if circumstances indicate reasonable trustworthiness of the information.[2]

Visual Observations

Observation of bulges in a suspect's clothing that are consistent with the likely presence of weapons may suggest just that, the presence of weapons. Typically, the observation of such a bulge in a suspect's clothing will be sufficient by itself to justify a protective frisk during a lawful stop.

Nature Of The Suspected Criminal Activity

Although the reasonable suspicion that justifies an investigative stop does not automatically justify a frisk, in some instances the very nature of the suspected criminal activity may suggest the presence of weapons. For example, officers normally would be justified in conducting a frisk of a person stopped on reasonable suspicion of armed robbery. The potential presence of weapons is reasonably inferred from the nature of the suspected criminal activity. In some areas, the same may be true in regard to street-level drug dealers.

The very nature of the suspected criminal activity may suggest the presence of weapons.

Discovery Of Weapons

When an officer observes a weapon in the vicinity of a person who has been lawfully stopped, the officer may reasonably suspect that other weapons are present and pose a threat. It is usually reasonable for an officer to take preventive measures to ensure that there are no other weapons within the person's reach.

Officer Knowledge Of Area And/Or Groups

Officers often have considerable knowledge and/or experience regarding certain places and/or groups. For example, an officer familiar with a neighborhood may know that an illegal nightclub is well known for its armed patrons, and would be entitled to take that fact into consideration in deciding whether to frisk a patron who is detained while coming out of the nightclub. In *United States v. Patton*, 705 F.3d 734 (7th Cir. 2013), a lawfully detained suspect's late-night presence in an area known by officers for gang activity as well as the location's proximity to the site of a drive-by shooting two nights prior established reasonable suspicion of the presence of a weapon on the suspect.

Suspect Behavior

> **Suspicious movements and other non-verbal behavior may sometimes be a basis for suspecting that weapons are present.**

Suspicious movements and other non-verbal behavior may sometimes be a basis for suspecting that weapons are present. The failure to comply with an officer's command to remove one's hand from a pocket might reasonably cause suspicion that a weapon is present. Extreme suspect nervousness may count toward reasonable suspicion of the presence of weapons in some situations.

Every so often, a court will draw the line on an officer's articulated basis of suspicion, perhaps as an effort to make a general statement to law enforcement personnel. For example, in *United States v. McKoy*, 428 F.3d 38 (1st Cir. 2005), a motorist was stopped in the daytime for a parking violation in a "high-crime" area, was nervous, avoided eye contact, and twice leaned toward the center console. The Court found that this combination of factors was not enough for a frisk. The decision is a good reminder that a number of behaviors that could point to the possible presence of weapons may be also consistent with ordinary citizen behavior in a contact with police, and that frisk searches are not automatically justified by nervous behavior. The particular problem in *McKoy* might have been solved for police by expanded articulation of training and experience – and consequent suspicion.[3]

Scope And Nature Of The Frisk Search

The frisk of a person may not go further than is necessary to accomplish its purpose. The sole object of a frisk is to determine whether a weapon is present and to neutralize the threat of physical harm to the officer and others. Therefore, the scope of the frisk is limited to the area from which weapons could be immediately accessed.

> *The frisk of a person may not go further than is necessary to accomplish its purpose.*

Quick accessibility is the key concept in determining the scope of a frisk search. For example, reaching into the instep of a high top tennis shoe is permissible as part of a frisk search, according to the Court in *United States v. Barboza*, 412 F.3d 15 (1st Cir. 2005). Generally the concept that frisks are limited to immediately accessible areas implies that no damage or breakage be done to belongings or containers carried by the subject. If one has to break open a container to reach its contents, those contents would not be considered immediately accessible.

During the frisk, manipulation of clothing and objects is allowed only to the extent necessary to confirm or dispel suspicion that an object is a weapon. Once a determination is made by the officer that the object is not a weapon, manipulation of that object as part of a frisk search must immediately cease, but the officer is not required to ignore sensory perceptions gained prior to that moment – the feel of drugs, for example.[4]

If, during lawful frisk activity, an officer feels something that is likely to be contraband or other evidence of crime, the officer may attempt to obtain consent from the person to retrieve the item or the officer may proceed under a different search theory, if available (probable cause theory, for example). Pursuant to frisk authority, the officer may remove any item or object that he reasonably believes to be a weapon. For example, in *United States v. Muhammad*, 604 F.3d 1022 (8th Cir. 2010), the Court admitted into evidence the results of a frisk where the officer removed a "hard object" that "felt like an item that could conceal a weapon" from the suspect's back pocket. If the object or item removed is not a weapon but is immediately apparent to be evidence of a crime, it may be seized under the plain view doctrine of warrantless seizure (discussed in Chapter 10 of this book).

> **Scenario #58** A police officer detains John Smith on reasonable suspicion that he just committed an armed robbery. Due to the fact that a firearm was used in the offense, the officer is justified in conducting a frisk of John for weapons. John is wearing a backpack that is zipped shut.
>
> Question: May the officer unzip the backpack to check for weapons?
>
> Answer: It depends on the type of backpack. If an exterior "pat down" of the backpack would sufficiently determine the presence or absence of a weapon, then no. If hard casing or other objects inside prevent that determination, the officer may unzip the backpack and glance inside to assure that there is no immediately accessible weapon.

The "Plain Feel" Doctrine

As mentioned earlier, an alternative theory that justifies many search and seizure actions is "probable cause." An officer is not required to ignore what the officer perceives through the sense of touch.[5] This "plain feel" concept is consistent with the general principle that probable cause may be based, in whole or in part, on the sensory perceptions of an officer as interpreted in light of the officer's training and experience. Therefore, if an officer touches an object during a lawful frisk search, determines that the item is not a weapon but perceives through the sense of touch that the item likely is contraband, the officer may make a warrantless seizure of that item based upon probable cause. The legal theory justifying this warrantless intrusion may be either exigent circumstances or search incident to arrest.

> Scenario #59 During a lawful frisk of a suspect, a police officer feels an object in the suspect's shirt pocket that he immediately, reasonably, believes to be a crack pipe.
>
> Question: May the officer reach into the suspect's pocket and retrieve the item?
>
> Answer: Yes. The officer may retrieve the object because it is immediately apparent to him to be contraband and, in making that determination, the officer did not exceed the bounds of a lawful frisk.

Exigent Circumstances (Probable Cause) Searches Of Persons

"Exigent circumstances" is a clearly-established exception to the search warrant requirement and may be used in situations where an officer has probable cause to believe that a person located in a public place is in possession of contraband or other evidence of crime. In such circumstances, a warrantless, probable cause-based, exigent circumstances search would be lawful because of the inherent mobility of the evidence and the likelihood the evidence and the suspect would be gone if the officer left to obtain a search warrant.[6]

What about detaining the suspect while a search warrant is being sought? Usually, the time that would pass while the warrant is being obtained would render the detention an arrest. Fortunately for police, with respect to possession of contraband, the same probable cause that could be used to obtain a search warrant usually would also form the basis for a probable cause arrest and associated search incident to arrest. Either exigent circumstances or search incident to arrest would furnish the warrantless search justification in such situations.

NOTE: the term "exigent circumstances" has different (and less demanding) meaning here and in vehicle searches than it does in connection with entries and searches of homes.

> **The same probable cause that could be used to obtain a search warrant usually would also form the basis for a probable cause arrest and associated search incident to arrest.**

> Scenario #60 A police officer arrives at the scene of a shoplifting complaint. The owner of the store tells the officer that he witnessed John Smith take a CD and put it in his coat pocket. The owner points out John, who is sitting outside the store. The officer approaches John. He denies shoplifting and refuses to allow the officer to search him. The officer nonetheless reaches into John's coat pocket and pulls out a CD.
>
> Question: Is this a lawful search?
>
> Answer: Yes. The officer had probable cause to believe that John was in possession of stolen property – that evidence of crime was on this person who was in public.

Special Needs Searches

The Supreme Court has recognized several situations occurring just beyond standard law enforcement activities that require a modified police response. These exceptional circumstances form the "special needs" exception to the warrant requirement. "Special needs" searches arise in tasks that are similar to the business of law enforcement but are more administrative in nature, such as searches in public schools and airports, and searches of persons on probation or parole. Typically, police get involved in these situations when an administrator or other non-law enforcement authority requests police assistance. In these situations, police may be able to assist a person whose authority to search is less restricted.

School Searches

Public school officials do not need a search warrant or even probable cause to conduct a search on public school grounds. Because of the need to provide safe environments for students, the Supreme Court has determined that school administrators' searches do not have to meet the search warrant and probable cause requirements that govern police searches. In *New Jersey v. T.L.O.*, 469 U.S. 325 (1985), the Court specifically authorized school administrators to search a student "when there are reasonable grounds for suspecting that the search will turn up evidence that the student has violated or is violating either the law or the rules of the school." When police officers are specifically assigned to work in a school and conduct searches in that capacity, the majority of courts apply the *T.L.O.* standard to their school-related searches.[7] Police officers who come to the school in their usual law enforcement capacity (i.e. to investigate a crime), must continue to operate within their usual "probable cause" standard and search warrant requirements.

Private schools are not "government" and the federal constitution does not regulate them at all. Private schools are regulated by contractual agreements between the students (or their parents) and the school, and the school's authority to search students and their belongings should be spelled out in their contractual agreement. Private enrollment agreements may give private school officials consent to search students and authority to exercise more control over students than is permitted in public schools.

Scenario #61 A police officer is called by school officials to a local high school. The school wants to conduct searches of students' vehicles in the school parking lot and wants the officer to actively participate in searching the vehicles.

Question: Is it lawful for the officer to participate in the search in this capacity?

Answer: No, unless the officer has probable cause or consent for each vehicle he searches, he may not actively participate in the searches. The school may be able to do administrative searches, but police cannot use police power to do them without ordinary constitutional justification.

Airport Searches

Airport searches in security areas are permitted without probable cause or even suspicion because passengers agree to subject themselves and their belongings to these administrative searches whenever they travel through these areas of airports. The heightened security needs in airports justify administrative measures – searches designed to detect weapons or explosives – and passengers agree to subject themselves to these searches. These searches are sometimes conducted by officials who have special authority to search passengers and their belongings on airport grounds, and they generally do not have law enforcement powers outside of the airport setting. The use of canines to sniff luggage in public areas does not constitute a search and is permitted without probable cause or reasonable suspicion.

Searches Of Probationers And Parolees

Recognizing the "special needs" of probation and parole systems, the Supreme Court has approved state laws that permit law enforcement searches of probationers and parolees without warrants and with less than probable cause.[8] The Court balances the government's interest in supervising this higher risk population of parolees and probationers against the reduced expectation of privacy that their status brings, and concludes these searches meet the "reasonable" search requirement of the Fourth Amendment. In *Griffin v. Wisconsin*, 483 U.S. 868 (1987), the Supreme Court applied the "special needs" doctrine to uphold a state regulation permitting a warrantless search of a probationer's home based on "reasonable grounds" to believe the police would find contraband. In a later application of the "special needs" doctrine, the Court said a warrantless search grounded in "reasonable suspicion" was reasonable under the Fourth Amendment, based on the diminished expectation of privacy of his status as a probationer.[9]

A parolee's expectation of privacy is even more reduced because he is usually under the supervision of a prison system. A "suspicionless" search of a parolee, based on the officer's knowledge of his status as a parolee, was allowed under a California law permitting police to search a parolee "with or without a search warrant and with or without cause" but prohibiting searches that are "arbitrary, capricious, or harassing."[10] To the extent that a probationer or parolee has explicitly waived specific Fourth Amendment rights as a condition of probation or parole, it may well be that resulting "suspicionless" searches by police are entirely lawful as long as they do not amount to harassment.

> **A parolee's expectation of privacy is even more reduced because he is usually under the supervision of a prison system.**

Police officers should verify the status of probationers and parolees with respect to their specific conditions of probation or parole by contacting appropriate probation and parole officers and should not assume that all probationers and parolees are subject to suspicionless searches.

> Scenario #62 A police officer sees a person the officer knows to be a parolee and the officer also knows the subject is under a condition of parole that he submit to warrantless searches by police, with or without particular justification. The officer stops the subject, explains what is happening, and without asking for consent conducts a warrantless search without probable cause or even reasonable suspicion.
>
> Question: Is this a lawful search?
>
> Answer: Yes. This person consented to this search as a condition of his parole.

Search Incident To Arrest

A search incident to arrest is a full and complete search for evidence and weapons within the area of immediate control of the arrestee. The landmark Supreme Court decision on search incident to arrest is *Chimel v. California*, 395 U.S. 752 (1969). Under *Chimel*, search incident to arrest is permitted automatically pursuant to every lawful arrest. The search must be conducted "substantially contemporaneously" with the arrest, and may even precede announcement of arrest.[11]

While probable cause is required for the arrest itself, a search incident to arrest may be conducted whether or not there is any reason to believe evidence and/or weapons will be found.[12] However, there must be a custodial arrest before there can be a search incident to an arrest. In *Knowles v. Iowa*, 525 U.S. 113 (1998), the Supreme Court held that issuance of a traffic citation, even for an arrestable offense, does not justify a search incident to arrest. At least one federal appeals court has limited the *Knowles* rule to traffic citations and allowed a "search incident to citation" of a pedestrian.[13] However, there is no trend supporting the approach taken by this Court.

> Scenario #63 John Smith is arrested on an outstanding warrant for failing to pay child support.
>
> Question: May the arresting officer conduct a full search of John, incident to his arrest?
>
> Answer: Yes. The nature of the offense of arrest is irrelevant when conducting a search incident to arrest. As long as there is a lawful, full-custody arrest, a search incident to arrest is also lawful.

Scope Of Search Incident To Arrest

A search incident to an arrest is a full search and may extend to the person, his/her clothing and carried belongings, and other areas within the immediate control of the arrestee.

A search incident to an arrest is a full search and may extend to the person, his/her clothing and carried belongings, and other areas within the immediate control of the arrestee. For example, if the arrest occurs in a motel room, a search incident to arrest may be conducted of the area immediately surrounding the arrestee, and could include looking in drawers, closets, under furniture, and in other places that could have been quickly reached by the arrestee.[14] In the event that an arrestee wants or needs access to particular areas for his or her convenience and/or comfort, the officer may inform the arrestee that such access is conditional upon the arrestee's consent to a prior search by the officer of the areas to which access is requested.[15] If consent is withheld, the arrestee normally would be denied access to that particular area. Subsequent access to toilets and such then would be allowed in facilities where the subject did not have a reasonable expectation of privacy – public facilities, for example – where the officer could conduct a prior search of the area to be accessed by the arrestee.

The lower courts are somewhat divided over the issue of searching cell phones as a search in an incident to arrest, but the majority of courts permit officers to search messages and call logs within a cell phone when that data is easily accessible by a click or two.[16] The courts primarily justify searching data contained within the cell phone under the preservation of evidence doctrine – meaning officers can collect information from the contents of the phone in the same manner that they could collect evidence from any closed container that was in the possession of the arrestee. Unfortunately, the evolution of technology moves a great deal faster than the trial and appeals process. Questions of whether laptop and possibly other computers can be searched fully as part of a search incident to arrest are not yet answered.

In *Arizona v. Gant*, 556 U.S. 332 (2009), the Supreme Court clarified and restricted the authority of police to search a vehicle incident to the arrest of that vehicle's occupant, but the Court only addressed these limitations in the context of a vehicle-related arrest. While the Court's justifications for limiting vehicle searches would logically apply to non-vehicular arrest situations, such as hotel rooms and other private premises, the Court has been silent on that prospect. The safer view, of course, is to assume that the *Gant* rule applies to persons who have been arrested in private premises but have been taken from those premises and secured outside.

> Scenario #64 John Smith is arrested. He is carrying a suitcase at the time of his arrest.
>
> Question: May the arresting officer search the suitcase incident to arrest?
>
> Answer: Yes. A search incident to arrest authorizes a full search of a person's carried belongings.

Motor Vehicles And Searches Incident To An Arrest

If the arrestee is seized from within a motor vehicle, the search incident to arrest may extend to the accessible portions of the passenger compartment only if the arrestee is unsecured and within reaching distance of the passenger compartment at the time of the search, or if it is reasonable to believe that evidence relevant to the crime of arrest may be in the passenger compartment. *Arizona v. Gant* specifically warns against police intentionally having a suspect unsecured in the area of the vehicle as a ploy to justify searching the interior of the vehicle.[17] This restriction is discussed more fully in Chapter 4, Vehicle Stops and Searches.

Search Incident To Change Of Custody Or Location

A search incident to arrest is also authorized upon a change of custody, consistent with the Fourth Amendment's requirement that searches and seizures be reasonable. It is reasonable that the police officer acquiring custody of an arrestee be allowed to insure that his prisoner does not have a weapon and/or evidence hidden on or around him, even if another officer may have conducted an earlier search incident to arrest. Officers may also search arrestees after arriving at a subsequent location when it was necessary to transport them immediately.[18]

> *It is reasonable that the police officer acquiring custody of an arrestee be allowed to insure that his prisoner does not have a weapon and/or evidence hidden on or around him.*

Strip Searches/Body Cavity Searches

Full strip and/or body cavity searches are rarely allowed except pursuant to specific orders in search warrants or in certain jail intake procedures.[19] Strip searches and visual body cavity inspections should be reserved for truly exigent circumstances involving high levels of probable cause to believe that weapons and/or critical evidence of serious crimes are present and that the only means reasonably available to remove the threat of access by the arrestee is to conduct such a search. In such cases, the officer should make every reasonable effort to maximize the personal privacy of the arrestee. The search should be conducted by an officer of the same gender as the arrestee, if reasonably possible. Partial strip searches, which involve manipulation of clothing without causing nudity, tend to be effective substitutes for full strip searches.

Body cavity intrusions are authorized only upon very high levels of focused probable cause to believe a weapon or evidence of crime is concealed in the body cavity. Absent consent or dire exigent circumstances compelling immediate warrantless action, body cavity probes should be performed pursuant to a

> *Body cavity intrusions are authorized only upon very high levels of focused probable cause to believe a weapon or evidence of crime is concealed in the body cavity.*

search warrant and only by qualified medical personnel. A visual inspection of the inside of the mouth probably would not be considered a cavity probe.

> Scenario #65 A police officer arrests Jane Smith for a drug offense and is conducting a search incident to arrest. The officer knows that Jane frequently carries contraband in her bra. The officer, a female, lifts the front of Jane's bra slightly and a crack pipe falls out. This is done in a manner that does not expose Jane's skin to public view.
>
> Questions: Is this a strip search and is this action permissible?
>
> Answer: The manipulation of Jane's bra was not a strip search and the action was permissibly part of a search incident to arrest.

Search And Inventory Of Personal Possessions Of A Person In Custody

In *Illinois v. Lafayette*, 462 U.S. 640 (1983), the Supreme Court made clear that it is reasonable to inventory the carried possessions of a person upon his or her entry into a detention facility. The primary justification for this action is the caretaking responsibility of law enforcement agencies in regard to the valuables and possessions of arrestees. The inventory assures that valuables are identified and safeguarded and helps protect against claims of theft or mismanagement of property. Lastly, the inventory protects officers and the detention facility against introduction of dangerous instrumentalities such as bombs, toxic materials, etc. In order for an inventory search to be lawful, the arrest and commitment into the detention facility must be lawful and there must be departmental policy requiring such an inventory. In *United States v. Edwards*, 415 U.S. 800 (1975), the Supreme Court held that a "second look" at areas and/or items previously searched may be permitted during continuous custody.

It is reasonable to inventory the carried possessions of a person upon his or her entry into a detention facility.

> Scenario #66 A police officer arrests John Smith and conducts a search incident to arrest. The only item in his pockets was his wallet. The officer looks in the wallet but does not find any contraband. Upon arrival at the jail, the officer decides to take another look in John's wallet. This time, he finds a small baggie of cocaine.
>
> Question: Was the second search of the wallet lawful?
>
> Answer: Yes. The officer is permitted to take a second look at items in the arrestee's possession so long as the arrestee remains in the officer's custody between the two searches.

NOTES

[1] *Arizona v. Johnson*, 555 U.S. 323 (2009).

[2] *But see Florida v. J. L.*, 529 U.S. 266 (2000).

[3] *See United States v. Soares*, 521 F.3d 117 (1st Cir. 2008), where a frisk in a similar situation was lawful, based upon the detailed facts provided by the officers.

[4] *Minnesota v. Dickerson*, 508 U.S. 366 (1993). *See also United States v. Bustos-Torres*, 396 F.3d 935 (8th Cir. 2005), where the officer felt "wads of cash" during a weapons frisk of a suspected street drug dealer.

[5] *See Minnesota v. Dickerson*, 508 U.S. 366 (1993).

[6] *See, for example, United States v. Banshee*, 91 F.3d 99 (11th Cir. 1996).

[7] *See New Jersey v. T.L.O.*, 469 U.S. 325 (1985), and *In the Matter of D.D.*, 554 S.E. 2d 346 (N.C. 2001).

[8] *Griffin v. Wisconsin*, 483 U.S. 868 (1987).

[9] *United States v. Knights*, 534 U.S. 112 (2001).

[10] *Samson v. California*, 547 U.S. 843 (2006).

[11] *Rawlings v. Kentucky*, 448 U.S. 98 (1980); *see also United States v. Smith*, 389 F.3d 944 (9th Cir. 2004) and *United States v. Powell,* 2007 WL 1119641 (D.C. Cir. 2007)(en banc) for recent applications of this principle.

[12] *United States v. Robinson*, 414 U.S. 218 (1973).

[13] *United States v. Pratt*, 355 F.3d 1119 (8th Cir. 2004).

[14] *See, for example, United States v. Currence*, 446 F.3d 554 (4th Cir. 2006), where a search incident to arrest properly included taking the handlebar caps off of the bicycle the arrestee was riding.

[15] *Washington v. Chrisman*, 455 U.S. 1 (1982).

[16] *See United States v. Finley*, 477 F.3d 250 (5th Cir. 2007), and *United States v. Murphy*, 552 F.3d 405 (5th Cir. 2011) and *United States v. Finley,* 477 F.3d 250 (5th Cir. 2007). *But see also United States v. Wurie*, 724 F.3d 255 (1st Cir. 2013) for an example of a court refusing to permit such searches.

[17] *Arizona v. Gant*, 556 U.S. 332 (2009).

[18] *See United States v. Avila-Dominguez*, 610 F.2d 1266 (1980), where searches took place at the courthouse rather than the site of arrest.

[19] *See, for example, Way v. County of Ventura*, 445 F.3d 1157 (9th Cir. 2006).

CHAPTER 9

NON-SEARCHES: OPEN FIELDS AND WOODS, AND ABANDONMENT

A "search" is an intrusion upon a "reasonable expectation of privacy." For a privacy expectation to be "reasonable," it must be one that society recognizes as such. An individual person might subjectively feel an expectation of privacy but not have one objectively, because under the circumstances the expectation of privacy would be objectively unreasonable.

Police actions that do not intrude on reasonable privacy expectations or possessory interests in property are neither searches nor seizures and do not implicate the Fourth Amendment. Some such actions involve the type of "looking around" by police that in lay definition would be called "searches"; however, in the constitutional sense they are "non-searches" because they do not intrude upon reasonable privacy expectations.

Police actions that do not intrude on reasonable privacy expectations or possessory interests in property are neither searches nor seizures and do not implicate the Fourth Amendment.

Open Fields And Woods

The best way to discuss the concept of "open fields and woods" may be to study a fact situation. Suppose a person buys a 100-acre plot of land and builds a house in the middle of the land in a grove of trees. He then surrounds the property with a barbed wire fence, the type normally used to keep farm animals contained. This person then posts "no trespassing" signs every 25 feet, all the way around the property. A gate is placed on the driveway; the gate has openings on each side which will allow people to enter but keep farm animals inside.

Under these circumstances many people would feel a subjective expectation of privacy in regard to the interior portions of this acreage. However, there is no constitutionally-protected privacy expectation in the property except for that portion of the property which immediately surrounds the home. The Supreme Court has held that the outlying areas are "open fields and woods" despite fencing and other barriers. The "no trespassing" signs may create a criminal or civil obligation but they do not create a reasonable expectation of privacy protected by the Fourth Amendment.[1]

The area that immediately surrounds the home is called the "curtilage." This concept contrasts with that of "open fields and woods." Curtilage typically receives Fourth Amendment privacy protection but "open fields and woods" do not. Consequently, one must understand where one ends and the other begins.

Curtilage normally equates to the "yard." Not all farmland would be considered the yard of the farmhouse even though the farmland surrounds the farmhouse. Privacy interests inside one's home receive the maximum protection of the Fourth Amendment. The area immediately surrounding the home (curtilage) gets privacy protection that is similar but not identical. Areas surrounding buildings that are seldom used, and non-secure buildings that are non-dwellings located within open fields and woods are not protected in the same ways.[2]

When a law enforcement officer walks onto private rural property, perhaps through a gate, passing through open fields and woods toward a residence, he will reach a point where the curtilage begins. An intrusion upon or into the curtilage may be considered a search and therefore may require Fourth Amendment justification, such as probable cause, a search warrant, exigent circumstances, or consent. In *Florida v. Jardines*, 133 S. Ct. 1409 (2013), the Supreme Court held that when a police officer brings a drug detection canine onto the curtilage of a home without a warrant or consent, he has intruded upon a constitutionally-protected area. Several factors are considered when determining if portions of a property are curtilage:

Proximity to the home: The closer the area is to the home, the more likely it is to be curtilage.

Enclosures associated with the home: Privacy screens, interior fences or thick bushes, often define the yard and are often indicators of curtilage.[3]

Nature and use of the area: If the area or outbuilding is used for purposes normally associated with family life, such as a garage or carport where the family car is normally parked, the area is likely to be curtilage.[4]

Not all entries onto curtilage are intrusions upon this constitutionally-protected area or reasonable privacy expectations. The use of common entranceways such as driveways or walkways to go directly to a front door usually does not amount to Fourth Amendment intrusion. These are the entranceways used by

> **Privacy interests inside one's home receive the maximum protection of the Fourth Amendment.**

those who would go to the door to knock or deliver packages or mail for example. Because they are commonly used, it would be unreasonable to expect privacy in regard to visual or other sensory observations from those pathways.[5] Some courts have held that it is permissible for officers to go into a backyard to knock on a back door where they are responding to a call, the home is apparently occupied, but no one responds to the officer's knocking at the front door.[6]

A nonconsensual entry into a secure building within open fields and woods is likely to be considered a search.[7] However, if the windows or door were left open, it would not be a search to look into the interior of a barn through those openings. However, looking through an open back door of a home from inside the fenced-in back yard would be a search because there is a reasonable expectation of privacy within the curtilage that protects against such a visual observation.[8]

A nonconsensual entry into a secure building within open fields and woods is likely to be considered a search.

The concepts of open fields and woods and curtilage are not hard and fast absolutes and must be considered in light of the totality of the circumstances.[9] Ultimately, resolution involves a common-sense judgment as to which concept applies to the area in question and as to the reasonableness of any expectation of privacy. Unfortunately, the law in this area is not crystal clear or entirely logical.

Scenario #67 A police officer arrives at a home to attempt to serve an arrest warrant on a resident. He proceeds directly to the front door and knocks. There is no answer and no indication that anyone is home. The officer then walks around to the rear of the home and notices that the back yard is surrounded by a six-foot tall privacy fence. The officer peers over the top of the fence and notices several marijuana plants growing in the back yard.

Question: Has the officer conducted a lawful search in discovering the marijuana plants?

Answer: No. He conducted an unlawful search when he peered over the fence since he intruded upon the owner's reasonable expectation of privacy in the curtilage of his home and, without any reason to believe the prospective arrestee was present, the warrant did not authorize entry or search.

Abandoned Personal Property

"Abandoned" property is not protected by the Fourth Amendment because it does not involve a reasonable expectation of privacy. The signs of property being abandoned are often matters of common sense. When property is discarded, thrown away, left unattended, unprotected and exposed to the public, it often becomes unreasonable to expect privacy in regard to that property. Such a forfeiture of one's reasonable expectation of privacy is an abandonment. Once property is abandoned, it is not a search for a law enforcement officer to inspect it, and no Fourth Amendment justification is required.

> Scenario #68 A police officer is in lawful foot pursuit of a suspect wearing a backpack. During the pursuit, the suspect throws the backpack in some bushes and continues running. The suspect gets away. The officer retrieves the backpack.
>
> Question: May the officer search the backpack without a warrant?
>
> Answer: Yes. The suspect abandoned the backpack during the course of a lawful police action; therefore, the officer may examine its contents without any other legal justification.

Abandonment Of Residential Property

Residential property is abandoned only if it is clearly unoccupied and shows obvious signs of non-use, such as broken windows, open doors, no power connections, etc.

In general, residential property is abandoned only if it is clearly unoccupied and shows obvious signs of non-use, such as broken windows, open doors, no power connections, etc. Usually, in such circumstances there would be no reasonable expectation of privacy in the property.

Where a person has rented a hotel or motel room but checkout time has come and gone, so has his reasonable expectation of privacy.[10] This rule might not apply where a person has merely held his room a few hours beyond the required checkout time or where there exists a practice of allowing guests to "stay over."[11] For an apartment or other longer-term rental property to be considered abandoned, the renter must have clearly vacated the apartment or been evicted by lawful authority and process.[12]

> Scenario #69 A police officer believes an "abandoned" house is currently being used for illegal drug activity. The windows on the house are broken out, there is no power to the building, the lawn is very overgrown and the front door is swinging in the breeze.
>
> Question: Does the officer need a search warrant to enter the building and investigate the suspected illegal activity?
>
> Answer: No. The current condition of the building makes it reasonable to assume that it has been abandoned – that no one has a reasonable expectation of privacy in this place.

Abandonment Of Vehicles

The Fourth Amendment's concept of abandonment is not necessarily the same as "abandoned vehicles" under state and local laws allowing removal of vehicles for reasons of public health, safety, or aesthetics. The signs of abandonment in the constitutional sense are much like those discussed above regarding residential property. The location of the vehicle will often be a guiding factor. For example, in *United States v. Gillis*, 358 F.3d 386 (6th Cir. 2004), a federal appeals court found no reasonable expectation of privacy in a wrecked and unlocked vehicle in a driveway but so close to the street that anyone walking down the street could have easily reached into the car.[13]

Trash, Garbage, And The Abandonment Rule

When trash has been placed in a public area for pick up, a reasonable expectation of privacy in the trash no longer exists. When a person who lives in an apartment complex puts his garbage into a plastic bag, carries that bag to the common dumpster and deposits it inside, the contents of the bag thereafter may be inspected without Fourth Amendment implications because there

When trash has been placed in a public area for pick up, a reasonable expectation of privacy in the trash no longer exists.

is no longer a reasonable expectation of privacy in the contents of the bag. Because the garbage bag is considered to be abandoned, the inspection of the contents would not be a search.[14] When a trash can is placed for pickup on the curb next to the street although still on the curtilage, it generally becomes unreasonable to expect privacy in its contents.[15] The contents would be considered abandoned. However, a trash can located next to the house and not yet "put out" by the street, may still involve a reasonable expectation of privacy. Examination of the contents would be a search requiring consent or other Fourth Amendment justification.[16]

NOTE: *This is an area where a number of states have created state law that is more restrictive than the federal principles stated above.*

Scenario #70 A police officer in a residential subdivision looks through the garbage in a trash can that has been placed by the curb for pick up. In the garbage, the officer finds suspected drug paraphernalia. He decides to attempt to obtain a search warrant for the residence based upon the evidence he found in the garbage.

Question: Has this officer already violated the resident(s)' rights by looking through their garbage?

Answer: No. When the garbage was put by the curb for pick up, it was abandoned and there was no longer any reasonable expectation of privacy.

Abandonment By Verbal Or Non-Verbal Interaction

Suppose an officer who suspects that a person may be transporting cocaine in a briefcase simply walks up to that person, identifies himself as a police officer, and asks the subject if the briefcase is his. The person says the briefcase is not his, places it on the ground, and walks away from it. The officer calls out, "Do you know whose it is?" The person responds, "It's not mine and I don't know whose it is." The officer may now open the briefcase without a search warrant or other Fourth Amendment justification because the possessor has voluntarily relinquished any once-held reasonable expectation of privacy in the now abandoned briefcase.[17] State law, though, is often stricter in this area, with state appeals courts often find no abandonment on similar facts.

For such an abandonment, there must be an affirmative denial of ownership and possessory interest. If that occurs, and if the object is located in an area where there is no other reasonable expectation of privacy, the object may be opened and inspected without satisfaction of usual Fourth Amendment requirements. In those situations where the totality of circumstances suggests that someone else may have a reasonable expectation of privacy in the item in question, special care must be taken to ensure that any abandonment comes from the right person or persons. Although the bag may be near one person, the bag may actually belong to someone else standing nearby or someone who is not present at all. For example, society would generally recognize an ongoing reasonable expectation of privacy in luggage that is still within the control and caretaking function of a common carrier such as a bus company – even if the item has been placed in a luggage retrieval area and persons nearby disclaim interest in the item.[18] Of course, where someone clearly discards or intentionally leaves behind an item in a public area, it is abandoned.[19]

Where someone clearly discards or intentionally leaves behind an item in a public area, it is abandoned.

> Scenario #71 A police officer at an airport has a hunch that a specific piece of luggage from an arriving flight contains contraband. The piece of luggage has been left unclaimed at the baggage carrousel. There is no one around the carrousel.
>
> Question: May the officer now open the luggage and inspect its contents?
>
> Answer: No. The owner has not relinquished his expectation of privacy regarding his luggage. Society would not generally recognize that an unclaimed piece of airline luggage at a baggage carrousel has been abandoned by its owner. Airline luggage is frequently lost or misplaced by the airline. The officer would need to obtain a search warrant in this case but seems to lack probable cause for one.

NOTES

[1] See *Oliver v. United States*, 466 U.S. 170 (1984) and, for background, *Hester v. United States*, 265 U.S. 57 (1924).

[2] See, e.g. *United States v. Barajas-Avalos*, 377 F.3d 1040 (9th Cir. 2004).

[3] See, e.g. *United States v. Mathias*, 721 F.3d 952. (8th Cir. 2013), where an 18-inch strip of private property located outside of a privacy fence was deemed not to be curtilage.

[4] *United States v. Dunn*, 480 U.S. 294 (1987).

[5] See, for example, *United States v. French*, 291 F.3d 945 (7th Cir. 2002).

[6] See, for example, *Hardesty v. Hamburg Township*, 461 F.3d 646 (6th Cir. 2006).

[7] See *United States v. Pennington*, 287 F.3d 739 (8th Cir. 2002).

[8] See *Dunn*, above, and *Daughenbaugh v. City of Tiffin*, 150 F.3d 594 (6th Cir. 1998).

[9] See, for example, *United States v. Bausby*, 720 F.3d 652 (8th Cir. 2013), where a front yard containing a motorcycle with an affixed "For Sale" sign was not deemed to be curtilage.

[10] *United States v. Kitchens*, 114 F.3d 29 (4th Cir. 1997).

[11] Compare *United States v. Dorais*, 241 F.3d 1124 (9th Cir. 2001), where guest's expectation of privacy was extended to 12:30 p.m. but not to 12:40 p.m., and *United States v. Lanier*, 636 F.3d 228 (6th Cir. 2011), noting that a hotel's practices and communications may extend a guest's expectation of privacy beyond the usual checkout time. See also *United States v. Young*, 573 F.3d 711 (9th Cir. 2009), where hotel guest maintained a reasonable expectation of privacy after hotel staff discovered a gun in his room and deactivated his room key.

[12] See, for example, *United States v. Hoey*, 983 F.2d 890 (8th Cir. 1993).

[13] See *United States v. Ramirez*, 145 F.3d 345 (5th Cir. 1998), for a general discussion of these issues.

[14] *California v. Greenwood*, 486 U.S. 35 (1988).

[15] See *United States v. Bowman*, 215 F.3d 951 (9th Cir. 2000).

[16] But see *United States v. Segura-Baltazar*, 448 F.3d 1281 (11th Cir. 2006), where the Court held that such an expectation of

privacy no longer existed after sanitation workers picked up the trash at a regularly-scheduled time.

[17] See United States v. Sanders, 130 F.3d 1316 (8th Cir. 1997) for example.

[18] See United States v. Garzon, 119 F.3d 1446 (10th Cir. 1997).

[19] See United States v. Liu, 180 F.3d 957 (8th Cir. 1999).

CHAPTER 10

NON-SEARCHES: THE PLAIN VIEW DOCTRINE, SENSORY PERCEPTION AND ENHANCEMENT TOOLS

A search is a physical intrusion upon a constitutionally-protected area or upon a reasonable expectation of privacy. An intrusion upon a reasonable expectation of privacy may or may not involve a physical intrusion. It may occur without entering any private premises or touching any person or property. A search might be the utilization of a bugging device to hear a private conversation, the use of an unlikely vantage point to gain a visual observation into private premises, or the use of intrusive technology not in common public use. Such searches are government intrusions upon a concept – the reasonable expectation of privacy.

The Supreme Court has developed a two-part test for whether a privacy expectation is reasonable under the Fourth Amendment:

1. Did a person actually, in fact, expect privacy?

2. Does society recognize that person's expectation as being reasonable and legitimate?

In *Katz v. United States*, 389 U.S. 347 (1967), the Supreme Court stated a fundamental legal principle:

> "What a person knowingly exposes to the public, even in his own house or office, is not the subject of Fourth Amendment protection."

Law enforcement officers are permitted to take advantage of this principle in order to facilitate criminal investigations, but there are rules. What follows is a discussion of the most important of those rules.

The Plain View Doctrine

The "plain view doctrine," widely misunderstood and misused, is better described as the "plain view doctrine of warrantless seizure." For purposes of this discussion, the term "seizure" is defined as a significant or meaningful interference by government with a person's possessory interest in property. The plain view doctrine of warrantless seizure deals not just with seeing things, but with seizing them. Just because an officer can see an

The plain view doctrine of warrantless seizure deals not just with seeing things, but with seizing them.

item doesn't mean an immediate warrantless seizure is permitted. The plain view doctrine of warrantless seizure may be stated as follows:

An officer lawfully present in a given location who sees in plain view an item which is immediately apparent to be evidence of a crime may seize that item without a warrant provided no further intrusion upon a constitutionally-protected area or reasonable expectation of privacy is required in order to accomplish the seizure.

Suppose an officer walking down a common corridor outside a row of motel rooms looks into an uncurtained window and sees illegal drugs and related paraphernalia on a table. Most would agree that there is a reasonable expectation of privacy within a motel room; however, there is no reasonable expectation of privacy in what one knowingly exposes to the public. The question then becomes, "Is the room occupant knowingly exposing his activity in that room to public view?" In this case, the answer is "yes." Therefore, it would not be a search for a police officer to stand outside and look inside. This sensory perception is a "non-search"; it is often called a "plain view observation" but it does not involve the plain view doctrine of warrantless seizure.

The plain view doctrine of warrantless seizure has to do with seizing items, not just seeing them. When only seeing is involved, there is only one pertinent constitutional question: "Does anyone have a reasonable expectation of privacy in respect to this particular sighting?" If the answer is "no," the Fourth Amendment does not apply to the visual observation because it is neither search nor seizure. But for the officer in this hypothetical situation to enter the motel room to seize the evidence, he would have to comply with the Fourth Amendment, using either a warrant or an exception if one exists to the warrant requirement.

The plain view doctrine of warrantless seizure involves several requirements. First, the officer must be lawfully present in the position from which a plain view observation is made. Second, the item observed must be "immediately apparent" to be evidence of a crime.[1] "Immediately apparent" means there is, upon sighting, probable cause to believe it is evidence of a crime. If these two requirements are satisfied, the officer may

The item observed must be "immediately apparent" to be evidence of a crime.

seize the item, provided no further physical or privacy intrusion is required.[2] A further intrusion, for example, would be going from outside a motel room to inside the room. In the motel room scenario above, the officer making the plain view sighting was not in a position from which a seizure could be accomplished. An additional intrusion would be necessary to accomplish the seizure. The officer's sighting of items in "plain view" would provide probable cause but would not activate the plain view doctrine of warrantless seizure. The plain view doctrine of warrantless seizure is not legal authority for an officer to enter private premises.

The plain view doctrine of warrantless seizure is not legal authority for an officer to enter private premises.

A potentially confusing case in this area is the Supreme Court decision in *Minnesota v. Carter*, 525 U.S. 83 (1998), where an officer looked into an apartment window through the gaps in the closed window coverings and saw three men packaging drugs inside. Without addressing whether such an observation into an apartment would infringe upon a reasonable expectation of privacy, the Court held that two of the men, temporary visitors there for illegal commercial purposes, did not have a reasonable privacy expectation in that apartment. Therefore, the Fourth Amendment was not implicated, much less violated, with respect to those two men – but the resident would have standing to contest the police action and probably could do so successfully.

Basic "plain view" principles are operative with respect to entering motor vehicles. For example, consider the frisk of the passenger compartment of a lawfully-stopped vehicle based on reasonable suspicion that weapons are present. During the frisk, should an officer observe a bag of cocaine on the floor board of the car, the officer may utilize the plain view doctrine of warrantless plain view seizure to seize the cocaine. The officer was lawfully present in the vehicle, the cocaine was in plain view, the cocaine was immediately apparent to be evidence of a crime, and no further intrusion was necessary to effect the seizure. However, if an officer standing outside a vehicle parked on a street were to look into the car and see a bag of cocaine on the seat, the officer would have made a lawful plain view observation but a further intrusion (going into the car) would be required to accomplish the evidence seizure. That further intrusion would require

Fourth Amendment justification beyond the plain view doctrine. In this case, the "*Carroll* Doctrine" (the vehicle exception to the search warrant requirement) would be available.

Prior to 1990, the Supreme Court had held that the plain view doctrine required an officer's sighting to be "inadvertent" – unplanned, unanticipated. In *Horton v. California*, 496 U.S. 128 (1990), the Supreme Court eliminated the inadvertence requirement. Now an officer may use the plain view doctrine of warrantless seizure even when the officer observes items he was fully expecting to see, provided the seizure meets the other requirements of the doctrine.

Also important with respect to the plain view doctrine is the Supreme Court decision in *Arizona v. Hicks*, 480 U.S. 321 (1987). In that case, an officer was lawfully present in a home, based on consent. The officer noticed expensive-looking stereo equipment in the otherwise very inexpensive-looking quarters. The officer picked up a stereo item and turned it over in order to record the serial number for comparison to stolen property records. The Court determined that the officer's action was a warrantless search without probable cause, and not an application of the plain view doctrine. The serial number was not in plain view, and the object had to be moved and manipulated in order to see the serial number. Because the serial number had not been exposed to public view, it was within a reasonable expectation of privacy. The officer's intrusion upon that expectation of privacy was therefore a search, in this case unlawful for want of probable cause and a warrant.

Scenario #72 A police informant purchases cocaine from John Smith using a $50 bill that was marked by the police. The transaction was made in John's house. A few minutes later, the officer knocks on the door of John's house hoping that John will speak with him. The officer identifies himself as a police officer and John invites him inside. Once inside, the officer sees a $50 bill on the coffee table bearing the same mark that the officer had put on the bill that he gave the informant. The officer then picks up the $50 bill to examine it further.

> Question: Was it permissible for the officer to pick up and further examine the $50 bill?
>
> Answer: Yes. The item was immediately apparent to the officer as being evidence of a crime. He seized the item under the authority of the plain view doctrine.

Sensory Perceptions

Visual perceptions often have little to do with the plain view doctrine of warrantless seizure. The sense of sight or visual observation is only one of the five sensory perceptions available to an officer. When an officer, during the course of a lawful frisk for weapons, feels an item that is immediately apparent to the officer to be crack cocaine, the officer has used the sensory perception of touch or feel. Although the plain view doctrine of warrantless seizure is not available because an additional intrusion of going into the pocket is necessary, the sensory perception of touch may furnish probable cause to arrest and search.[3]

Sensory perceptions often require evaluation of the concept of reasonable expectation of privacy and application of the definition of search. In the *Hicks* case, above, the officer lifted a stereo component to see a part that had not been exposed to public view. That was a "search." The smelling of an odor coming from a building by an officer lawfully present on the exterior is not a search and may establish reasonable suspicion or even probable cause. There is generally no reasonable expectation of privacy regarding odors escaping into the public domain; therefore, smelling such an odor usually is not a search. The Fourth Amendment simply does not apply.

Similarly, most courts hold that the suspicion-less "running" of motor vehicle tag numbers is not a search because there is no reasonable expectation of privacy in heavily-regulated licenses that are exposed to public view.[4]

Understanding when sensory observations are and are not searches can be difficult. Consider an actual trial court decision where an officer received an anonymous tip that an individual was cutting drugs on a table inside a seventh-floor apartment.

There is no reasonable expectation of privacy in heavily-regulated licenses that are exposed to public view.

The window curtains were open. There were no other buildings nearby from which the officer could observe the interior of the suspected apartment so the officer went up a small mountain several miles away, used his binoculars, but could not see much detail. The officer then went to a nearby NASA station and borrowed a high-powered telescope. He returned to the mountain from which he could then clearly see the activities inside the suspected apartment. In fact, the officer could read the title of the paperback novel the suspect was reading at the time. The officer observed drugs, obtained a search warrant and, upon its execution, seized a large quantity of narcotics.

The case hinged on whether the observation from the mountainside with the high-powered telescope was a search regulated by the Fourth Amendment. In this case the Court held that the visual observations aided by the telescope were an illegal search. The residents of this seventh-floor apartment, though the curtains were wide open, had a reasonable expectation of privacy, considering that the only way to see in the windows was to station a high-powered telescope on a mountain several miles away. Therefore, the sensory perception of sight in this case would be a search requiring prior probable cause and a warrant. Generally, though, should the resident or occupant of a building choose to leave the curtains open although there is a public area or neighboring property from which someone can look into the building through the windows, there would not be reasonable expectation of privacy and such a visual observation from neighboring property would therefore be a "non-search."

> Scenario #73 A police officer stops a vehicle for a traffic violation. When he walks up to the car, he smells a very strong odor of what he immediately recognizes as marijuana coming from inside the vehicle.
>
> Question: May the officer search the vehicle without the consent of the driver?
>
> Answer: Yes. The officer has made a "plain smell" observation in a public area. He has developed probable cause to search the vehicle and he may do so without a warrant under the *Carroll* Doctrine.

Sensory Enhancement Tools

Enhancement tools are those used to increase or improve sensory perceptions and abilities. Examples include magnification and illumination devices like binoculars, telescopes, flashlights and night scopes. Drug and bomb sniffing dogs enhance the ability to detect certain odors. Certain microphones and audio equipment can enhance the ability to hear. Overflight surveillance from aircraft allows sightings that otherwise could not be made.

When determining whether use of a particular enhancement tool is lawful, an officer again must consider the concept of reasonable expectation of privacy. In respect to sight, if an unaided observation from the same location would be allowed, then enhancement tools usually are allowed. However, several questions must be considered:

Are the activities occurring in a public area? For these purposes, a public area includes parking lots, street corners, common areas of apartment complexes, and other locations where no one in particular has a reasonable expectation of privacy. In observing such areas, visual enhancement tools almost always are allowed, though oral communication might still be protected from audio surveillance by enhancement devices such as parabolic microphones. Consider the use of the telescope from the mountainside discussed earlier. Had the surveillance been of activity taking place on a street corner, the officer could have used the NASA telescope with no legal problems because there would be no intrusion upon a reasonable expectation of privacy.

Are the activities, though in a private area, knowingly exposed to public view? If activities are exposed to public view, there generally is no reasonable expectation of privacy and no Fourth Amendment problems with visual observations.

Does the observation require use of an enhancement device that is especially sophisticated or unusual? If the required enhancement device is uncommon in society, one might have a reasonable expectation of privacy based on the notion that a device of that kind was unlikely to be used. If a device is highly sophisticated and/or almost nobody has it, it might be reasonable to expect that it will not be used. In the case of *Kyllo v. United*

> When determining whether use of a particular enhancement tool is lawful, an officer again must consider the concept of reasonable expectation of privacy.

States, 533 U.S. 27 (2001), for example, the Court found that police use of a thermal imaging device to detect the heat signature of a home, even though the police and the device were not physically on the property or curtilage, was a search in and of itself. The decision relied significantly on the "uncommonness" of thermal imaging equipment and the fact that it could reveal non-criminal activity.[5]

Is the vantage point remote or unusual? The more remote and/or unusual the required vantage point, arguably the more reasonable is an expectation of privacy.

Generally, officers should not go onto the curtilage or yard of a private residence in order to gain sensory observations. Going onto a curtilage may be a search in and of itself. It is usually permissible, however, to use walkways that are in common public use. For example, an officer may use a commonly-traveled walkway to reach the front door of a private residence. A visual observation or other sensory perception made while on that walkway usually would not be considered a search, even though it was made from within the curtilage. (See the discussion of Open Field and Woods, at page 155) Courts are split on whether taking a drug detection canine to a bedroom door pursuant to another resident's consent is a search.[6]

> *The more remote and/or unusual the required vantage point, arguably the more reasonable is an expectation of privacy.*

Scenario #74 A police officer standing on a public street uses binoculars to peer into an un-curtained window of a residence. He can see a man inside the residence packaging drugs. The officer wants to use this observation as the basis for a search warrant for the residence.

Questions: Is the officer's use of binoculars to look into this home already a "search?" Does his action intrude upon the resident's reasonable expectation of privacy?

Answer: No. The man inside the residence has exposed his activities to public view by conducting the activity in front of an uncovered window. There is absolutely nothing that would be considered sophisticated or unusual about the use of binoculars. The use of binoculars merely allows the officer to get a better look at what the man has already exposed to public view.

General Notes On Surveillance, Enhancement Tools, And Electronic Eavesdropping

While the law in this is not completely clear or entirely logical, certain generalizations are possible. Binoculars are commonly available, so use of them is generally lawful. Flashlights and night scopes, like binoculars, are lawful in almost all circumstances. Using aircraft to fly over suspect locations to look down into an area generally does not implicate the Fourth Amendment even if sophisticated enhancement tools are used, at least as long as the aircraft remains in lawfully navigable airspace.[7] Use of telescopes may or may not be considered a search, depending on analysis of reasonable expectation of privacy discussed earlier. Use of scent detection canines in public areas is generally permissible.[8] However, bringing a scent detection canine on the curtilage of a home is a search.[9]

The installation and use of GPS-based tracking devices on vehicles involves a physical trespass onto a constitutionally-protected area and is therefore a search, according to the U.S. Supreme Court in *United States v. Jones*, 132 S. Ct. 945 (2012), but that case did not decide whether a prior warrant is required for such actions. Earlier Supreme Court decisions had approved similar warrantless surveillance using electronic "beepers" but those decisions are now questionable given the *Jones* decision.[10] At least until this issue is further clarified, the safer approach is to obtain a warrant to install and use such enhancement tools. In any event, prior probable cause is now clearly required.

The safer approach is to obtain a warrant to install and use such enhancement tools.

Wiretapping, electronic eavesdropping, etc., are generally prohibited under federal law unless state law permits. In those matters, inquiry into state law is essential. Federal law permits the interception of oral or wire communication as long as one party to the conversation consents to monitoring.[11] Some state law varies and requires notification and/or all party consent. The interception of oral communication in which there is a reasonable expectation of privacy is a federal felony.

> Scenario #75 A police officer stops a car for a traffic violation. He has a hunch that there may be drugs in the car. He calls for a canine officer to respond and begins writing the traffic ticket. The canine officer arrives two minutes later and begins to walk his dog around the exterior of the vehicle while the original officer completes the ticket writing. The dog alerts on the vehicle.
>
> Question: Has the use of the drug dog in this manner amounted to an unlawful search or contributed to an illegal seizure?
>
> Answer: No. The vehicle was lawfully stopped and during the course of the lawful detention, the dog merely walked around the exterior of the vehicle, an area where the driver has no expectation of privacy. It is important to remember, though, that, absent reasonable suspicion of drug activity, the duration of the detention may not be extended simply to allow time for the dog to arrive or to conduct its walk around the vehicle.

Summary

Proper analysis of these issues requires evaluation of each individual situation. There are few absolutes. If a visual observation is of activity occurring in an area where no one has a reasonable expectation of privacy, the observation generally would not be a search. If the activity is occurring within an area of reasonable expectation of privacy, visual observations may very well be a search and further consideration is required. Generally, the more remote or unusual the vantage point and the more sophisticated and unusual the enhancement tool(s), the more likely it is that the officer's actions would be considered a search requiring prior probable cause and a warrant.

NOTES

[1] *See United States v. Paneto*, 661 F.3d 709 (1st Cir. 2011) for a useful discussion of the "immediately apparent" requirement.

[2] *United States v. Brown*, 701 F.3d 120 (4th Cir. 2012).

[3] *But see Minnesota v. Dickerson*, 508 U.S. 366 (1993) and *Bond v. United States*, 529 U.S. 334 (2002), on when too much manipulation of an item itself becomes a search.

[4] *See, for example, United States v. Ellison*, 462 F.3d 557 (6th Cir. 2006) and *United States v. Diaz-Castaneda*, 494 F.3d 1146 (9th Cir. 2007).

[5] *See, for example, Kyllo v. United States*, 533 U.S. 27 (2001), where the Court found that police use of a thermal imaging device to detect the heat signature of a home, even from off the curtilage, was a search in and of itself. The decision relied significantly on the "uncommonness" of thermal imaging equipment and the fact that it could reveal non-criminal activity.

[6] *See, for example, United States v. Brock*, 417 F.3d 692 (7th Cir. 2005) and compare *United States v. Thomas*, 757 F.2d 1359 (1985).

[7] *See California v. Ciraolo*, 476 U.S. 207 (1986); *Dow Chemical v. United States*, 476 U.S. 227 (1986); and *Florida v. Riley*, 488 U.S. 445 (1989).

[8] *United States v. Place*, 462 U.S. 696 (1983); *Illinois v. Caballes*, 543 U.S. 405 (2005).

[9] *See Florida v. Jardines*, 133 S. Ct. 1409 (2013), where the Court relied on physical trespass theory though it might as easily found an intrusion into a reasonable expectation of privacy.

[10] *See United States v. Karo*, 468 U.S. 705 (1984) and *United States v. Knotts*, 460 U.S. 276 (1983) for how the law stood prior to *Jones*.

[11] *Hoffa v. United States*, 385 U.S. 293 (1966); *United States v. Lee*, 359 F.3d 194 (3d Cir. 2004).

CHAPTER 11

CONSENT TO SEARCH

Asking for consent to search is in fact asking a person to give up a reasonable expectation of privacy. If a valid consent is obtained, an officer may search the item or area in question without any other Fourth Amendment justification. Because it does not involve an intrusion upon a reasonable expectation of privacy, a "consent search" is really a non-search.

For a consent to be valid it must be voluntary, given without undue coercion or duress.[1] Officers may not threaten a person with police action in order to obtain consent to a search. However, a truthful statement like, "If you don't consent, I am going to apply for a search warrant," generally is permitted.[2] Stating "If you don't consent, I'm just going to get a search warrant and search anyway," is generally considered too coercive and invalidates a resulting consent.[3] In one case, the officer is stating something to be true that he or she controls – application for a search warrant. In the other, the officer is stating something to be true that is actually controlled by intermediary judicial decision-making – suggesting authority that does not yet exist. The differences are subtle but important.

> *For a consent to be valid it must be voluntary, given without undue coercion or duress.*

Deception To Obtain Consent

Courts, including federal courts, are divided on the questions of what types and degrees of deception are permitted in order for police to facilitate a consent process. Obviously, undercover work involves constant deception and often results in officers being admitted into private premises where, if the truth were known, they would never have been invited. Such scenarios rarely result in legal controversy – courts universally accept such undercover work and its necessary deceptions. "Misplaced confidence" does not violate the Constitution.[4] But what about officers posing as phone company employees going to someone's door and explaining a need to come in the house to check for a system problem? Or posing as gas company employees needing to check inside for hazardous conditions that purportedly represent an emergency threat to the safety of the residents? These are the questions which divide the courts – unfortunately, to the extent that no discernible trend can be identified. Creating a ruse outside private premises to draw occupants outside is generally permitted. False representation of legal authority to search voids a consent, according to *United States v. Escobar*, 389 F.3d 781 (8th Cir. 2004), where officers falsely claimed that a drug dog had alerted to the suspect's property. Falsely claiming to possess a search warrant will also void consent to search a residence.[5] Most courts agree in regard to false claims of legal authority. Creating a ruse in order to facilitate service of warrant is different, of course, and is generally permitted.[6]

> **False representation of legal authority to search voids a consent.**

Who Can Consent?

In general, a valid consent must be obtained from someone who has a reasonable expectation of privacy in the property to be searched. This means that an officer must reasonably believe that the person who is giving the consent to search has the authority to grant consent over the area or item in question. Usually, this involves common-sense judgments under the totality of the circumstances, but there may be very reasonable mistakes in this area. As long as the mistake is objectively reasonable, a resulting consent is still valid.[7]

> **Valid consent must be obtained from someone who has a reasonable expectation of privacy in the property to be searched.**

Generally, however, either spouse living in a home may consent to search of the areas commonly and mutually used.[8] Roommate situations are treated much like spouses. In either case, consent by one is invalid as to areas in which another person has exclusive privacy interests. In a case of huge importance, the Supreme Court decided in *Georgia v. Randolph*, 547 U.S. 103 (2006) that where both spouses are present at their home, one purportedly granting consent to enter and search and the other denying consent, the purported consent is insufficient and police may not enter based on it. One post-*Randolph* case applies the *Randolph* rule even where the objecting co-habitant is not physically present but is talking to police on the phone.[9]

A parent generally may consent to the search of the bedroom of a child.[10] However, there are situations where such a consent may not be valid. The factors courts consider include the child's age, whether there is regular access by the parent to the room, and/or whether rent is being paid by the child. The "child" could be an adult living in the parent's home. A "child" may reach an age and a status such that he may actually be able to give a valid consent to search the common area of a home, like spouses or roommates. Young children generally cannot validly consent to a search of their parents' home, although there is a federal appeals court decision saying a nine-year old could consent to entry.[11] It was crucial in that case that the "consent" only validated the officers' stepping inside the front door to wait for the arrival of an adult, and was not a consent to actually search the premises.

In almost all cases involving landlord-tenant relationships, the consent must be obtained from the tenant, the person with the reasonable expectation of privacy.[12] Thus, a landlord generally may not consent to the search of the tenant's residence, even if there is a lease provision that allows him to inspect the property for maintenance or other purposes.[13] A tenant may consent to a search of the property he rents even over the objections of the landlord.

In overnight house guest situations, the homeowner's consent is required for search of the house in general. However, the overnight house guest who has sole use of a bedroom has a reasonable expectation of privacy in that room. Consent to search that room must be obtained from the house guest.[14]

In an employer-employee situation, consent of the employer is generally adequate for workplace searches; however, employees may have a personal reasonable expectation of privacy in some areas within the workplace. Some employers reduce or eliminate reasonable privacy expectations of employees by notifying them that areas such as lockers, desks, and offices belong to the employer, are subject to inspection at any time, and that lock combinations must be filed with the employer. In such cases, the employer may conduct a "non-search" of an employee's "personal area" because, in fact, the employee does not have a reasonable expectation of privacy in that area. However, the way an area is actually used over a period of time can change the result.[15]

In owner-custodian relationships where the owner leaves an object in the care of another – at a valet-involved parking garage, for example – federal case law is unclear. Relevant questions include whether the custodian appears to have lawful authority

> *Young children generally cannot validly consent to a search of their parents' home.*

> *Consent of the employer is generally adequate for workplace searches; however, employees may have a personal reasonable expectation of privacy in some areas within the workplace.*

to access the areas as to which consent is being requested or his role is just "storage" of the object. An individual who has been granted access to or entrusted to care for property is *more likely* to be considered by courts to be able to validly give consent to the police to access the property. However, this "access authority" does not necessarily settle the issue of valid consent.[16]

> Scenario #76 A police officer responds to a residence in reference to a domestic disturbance. Upon arrival the officer speaks with a man who had been arguing with his wife, who left before the officer arrived. Husband and wife both reside at the residence and share use of all areas in it. Believing that the wife may be involved in drug activity, the officer asks the husband for consent to search the residence. The husband gives consent. Just as the officer begins the search, the wife arrives and tells the officer that she does not want him searching her home.
>
> Question: May the officer continue the search since he already had consent from the husband?
>
> Answer: No. Both the husband and the wife have a common interest in the property. Consent from one party may be overruled by the other party at any time.

Consent Considerations Arising Out Of An Officer's Language

Officers should ask for consent in a way that clearly indicates a real choice.

Officers should ask for consent in a way that clearly indicates a real choice, should make their requests clear, and may also wish to define the scope of the search they wish to conduct. When asking to search a vehicle, good words would be: "May I have permission to search you, your vehicle, and its contents?" In that case, there is no question that a consent to search is being requested for the person, the vehicle and the contents of the vehicle, and that the person has a choice.

Officers are not required to advise of the right to refuse consent.[17] However, there may be cases involving mental impairment, age, or other circumstances in which an officer would want to advise a person of his right to refuse so that the consent is strengthened.

A person who has been stopped need not be informed that he is free to leave in order to get a valid consent to a search. In *Ohio v. Robinette*, 519 U.S. 33 (1996), Robinette was stopped for traffic law violation. The officer asked for consent to search after issuing a warning and returning Robinette's driver's license, but without saying "You're free to leave." The resulting consent was valid, according to the Court.

Consents are not required to be in writing. Proving a valid consent requires testimonial credibility, whether or not a written form is used. Recording the consent conversation provides better documentation than does a form and is helpful, provided state law permits such recordings.

Officers are not required to describe what they are searching for in order to obtain a valid consent. However, if the officer does not identify small objects of search or request permission to conduct a "complete" search, the scope of the consent could be unclear; a resulting search could exceed the scope of the consent.[18] A person in lawful custody may give a valid consent provided no other coerciveness would render the consent involuntary.[19]

Officers are not required to describe what they are searching for in order to obtain a valid consent.

Scenario #77 A police officer arrives at John Smith's house to arrest him on an outstanding warrant. John is home and is arrested in his living room. After handcuffing him and telling him he is under arrest, the officer asks John nicely and non-coercively for permission to search his house for drugs. John consents.

Question: Given the fact that John is under arrest, is his consent to search his home valid?

Answer: Yes. A person under arrest can validly give consent so long as no coercive measures on the part of law enforcement were used.

The Consent Itself

Officers may wish to clarify any ambiguous response given by the person from whom consent is requested but a non-verbal gesture may be a sufficient consent under some circumstances.[20] Consent may be limited. Someone may allow an officer to search a car except for the trunk. He may limit the officer to three minutes searching time. Consent may be given and then revoked. The officer must abide by the limitations placed on the consent unless alternate legal justification exists for a search action.

Consent may be and often should be utilized in conjunction with Fourth Amendment justifications such as probable cause and search warrants. An officer who has probable cause to search a vehicle stopped on a public street may wish to obtain consent to search the vehicle, even though warrantless search is already authorized under another exception to the warrant requirement. A valid consent on top of the alternate search justification simply makes police victory in court more likely. If there is something wrong with the consent, the other justification is still viable, and vice versa.

Scenario #78 A police officer lawfully stops a vehicle and obtains from the driver a valid consent to search the vehicle. The officer asks the driver if he would mind sitting in the back of the officer's patrol car for a few minutes for safety reasons. The subject cheerfully agrees and is seated in the police car. The windows are rolled up and the door is locked. The officer the conducts the search of the subject's car.

Question: Is this a lawful consent search?

Answer: Yes, but there could be a problem here. The driver has the right to withdraw his consent at anytime. Although the officer is not required to tell him of his right to refuse or withdraw consent, it is best not to put him in a place where he can't be heard, lest he later claim that he was trying to withdraw his consent and was unable to do so because the officer limited his ability to communicate.

NOTES

[1] *Schneckloth v. Bustamonte*, 412 U.S. 218 (1973).

[2] *See Bumper v. North Carolina*, 391 U.S. 543 (1968) and *United States v. Garcia*, 890 F.2d 355 (11th Cir. 1989).

[3] *See United States v. Boukater*, 409 F.2d 537 (5th Cir. 1969).

[4] *Hoffa v. United States*, 385 U.S. 293 (1966); *Lewis v. United States*, 385 U.S. 206 (1966).

[5] *United States v. Shaw*, 707 F.3d 666 (6th Cir. 2013).

[6] *See, for example, United States v. Alejandro*, 368 F.3d 130 (2d Cir. 2004).

[7] *Illinois v. Rodriguez*, 497 U.S. 177 (1990).

[8] *See United States v. Matlock*, 415 U.S. 164 (1974) and *United States v. Solis*, 299 F.3d 420 (5th Cir. 2002).

[9] *United States v. Hudspeth*, 459 F.3d 922 (8th Cir. 2006).

[10] *See United States v. Rith*, 164 F.3d 1323 (10th Cir. 1999).

[11] *Lenz v. Winburn*, 51 F.3d 1540 (11th Cir. 1995).

[12] *See Chapman v. United States*, 365 U.S. 610 (1961).

[13] *See United States v. Warner*, 843 F.2d 401 (9th Cir. 1988).

[14] *Minnesota v. Olson*, 495 U.S. 91 (1990).

[15] *See, for example, O'Connor v. Ortega*, 480 U.S. 709 (1987).

[16] *See United States v. Basinski*, 226 F.3d 829 (7th Cir. 2000). For insights into who can consent to a search of computer files, see *United States v. Buckner*, 473 F.3d 551 (4th Cir. 2007); *United States v. Ziegler*, 474 F.3d 1184 (9th Cir. 2007); and *United States v. King*, 604 F.3d 125 (3d Cir. 2010).

[17] *United States v. Drayton*, 536 U.S. 194 (2002).

[18] For a discussion of this issue, see *Florida v. Jimeno*, 500 U.S. 248 (1991).

[19] *See United States v. Watson*, 423 U.S. 411 (1976) and *United States v. Burns*, 298 F.3d 523 (6th Cir. 2002), where a consent from a handcuffed person was found to be valid.

[20] *United States v. Drayton*, above. See also *United States v. Carter*, 378 F.3d 584 (6th Cir. 2004)(en banc) and *United States v. Sabo*, 724 f.3D 891 (7th Cir. 2013) for an application of *Drayton*.

CHAPTER 12

SEARCH WARRANTS

The law of search warrants is almost always a combination of federal constitutional principles and state law requirements. State law usually has much to say regarding search warrant application and execution procedures. This discussion focuses on federal constitutional requirements, while noting frequently recurring state law issues.

The Fourth Amendment to the United States Constitution states:

"The right of the people to be secure in their persons, houses, papers, and effects, against unreasonable searches and seizures, shall not be violated; and no warrant shall issue but upon probable cause, supported by oath or affirmation and particularly describing the place to be searched and the persons or things to be seized."

So, the Fourth Amendment requires that:

1. All search and seizures be "reasonable."

2. Warrants be based on "probable cause."

3. Warrants be supported by "oath or affirmation."

4. Warrants "particularly describe" the place to be searched and person or things to be seized.

The law of search warrants is almost always a combination of federal constitutional principles and state law requirements.

Exceptions To The Warrant Requirement

As earlier discussed, not every search and/or seizure requires a search warrant. There are a variety of searches that fall within well-established exceptions to the warrant requirement. Examples include frisks, searches incident to arrest, and inventory searches. Certain other police actions do not require a warrant because they are not searches as that term is defined in Fourth Amendment law. Examples include consent "searches," observations in open fields and woods, and certain other observations/perceptions in or of public areas.

The Benefits Of A Warrant

Where the law is unclear as to whether or not a warrantless search is permitted, officers might consider:

1. A search warrant will sometimes permit a more extensive search than would be the case if a warrantless search was conducted.

2. Obtaining a warrant often will help protect an officer from civil liability and/or criminal prosecution.

3. There is a procedural advantage in obtaining a warrant. The criminal defendant has the burden of showing lack of probable cause or other defect when trying to suppress evidence seized pursuant to a warrant. The prosecution has the burden of proving probable cause when searches and seizures are made without a warrant and of proving that the warrantless search was lawful.

4. Evidence seized pursuant to a warrant is sometimes admissible even when it is ultimately determined that probable cause was lacking. Under federal law, there is a partial "good faith" exception to the exclusionary rule when an officer reasonably relies on an apparently valid search warrant.[1]

5. "Anticipatory" search warrants – which become effective only upon the occurrence of a triggering event – may be useful occasionally.[2]

6. A number of states allow police to obtain search warrants by telephonic communication with judicial officials. This often sharply reduces the time and effort involved in obtaining a warrant and makes that option more practical and convenient.

Definitions Of Key Terms

What Is A Search Warrant?

A more accurate name for a search warrant would be a "search and seizure warrant."

A search warrant is a judicial order. Typically, it commands that a law enforcement officer (with territorial jurisdiction) conduct the search and seizure action(s) authorized by the warrant. A more accurate name for a search warrant would be a "search and seizure warrant" because nearly all search warrants order a seizure.

What Is A Seizure?

Generally, a seizure is either a significant governmental interference with someone's possessory interest in property, or the arrest or detention of a person. The thing to be seized, whether an item of property or a person, is almost always the ultimate goal of a search warrant.

What Is A Search?

A search is a governmental intrusion upon a constitutionally-protected area or upon a reasonable expectation of privacy. When an officer intrudes upon a reasonable expectation of privacy, a search warrant will be required, unless the action falls within a recognized exception to the search warrant requirement.

What Is Involved In Applying For A Search Warrant?

A search warrant application consists mainly of several descriptions and a probable cause statement. Every jurisdiction publishes forms that guide the application process.

The Descriptions In A Search Warrant

The Fourth Amendment explicitly requires that search warrants particularly describe both the places to be searched and the person(s) and/or thing(s) to be seized. This is the first major component of a search warrant application. If this requirement is not met, the warrant is constitutionally defective, resulting evidence will usually be suppressed, and liability exposures are created. There are actually three things that must be sufficiently described:

1. The Crime (that is believed to have occurred).
2. The Evidence (that is to be seized).
3. The Place (that is to be searched).

In describing the crime, it is best to use a plain-language reference even if a statute number or some other technical reference is used. That way, if a mistake is made with a number or

The Fourth Amendment explicitly requires that search warrants particularly describe both the places to be searched and the person(s) and/or thing(s) to be seized.

reference, there will still be a sufficient description of the crime. "Rape" would probably be a sufficient crime description. Adding the degree, type, statute number, or other technical reference bolsters the description and would be helpful to include. Date, place, and victim identifiers might be included as well.

In describing what is to be seized, the effort should be to describe the item or person well enough to make it unlikely that the wrong thing or person will be seized. Because all contraband is subject to seizure, looser descriptions are accepted when the items to be seized may not be lawfully possessed. So, for example, "cocaine" might be a sufficient description even though there was no description of the variety or packaging. To use such a generic description of an item that may be lawfully possessed (e.g. "television") generally would not be sufficiently particular, and more descriptive information would be required. If known, information should be included as to a person's name, age, race, gender, and as detailed a physical description as is available.

In describing the place to be searched, a rule of thumb should be considered: Describe the place well enough that a person unfamiliar with the case could take the description, go out into the world, and find the right place. Street numbers on houses, for example, are very easy to confuse and/or mistype. A physical description, if available, should be included to minimize the potential for mistake.[3] The same principle would apply to vehicle tag numbers and physical descriptions. If it is known that vehicles and outbuildings are to be included in a search of certain premises, they should be mentioned and described as well as possible. Such a warrant may allow searches of vehicles that arrive after the search has begun.[4]

The Probable Cause Statement

The second major component of a search warrant application is the probable cause statement. The key to success in writing a probable cause statement is organizing information on paper or electronically before writing out the probable cause statement and completing the application. Such an outline or worksheet might start this way:

1. List each item of information by date received.

2. For each item of information, identify the source(s).

3. In respect to each source, state why the source should be believed.

Addressing these issues in writing is the first step toward writing a good probable cause statement. Ultimately, the probable cause statement must link the crime, the place to be searched, and the evidence to be seized by credible information sufficient to form at least a fair probability that the evidence to be seized is in the place to be searched.

Why Should The Information Be Believed?

For purposes of this discussion, "hearsay" is information from a source other than the officer's personal observations. For all hearsay information in a search warrant application, there ideally will be information showing:

1. How the source obtained the information; and

2. Why the hearsay source should be believed.

Prior to *Illinois v. Gates*, 462 U.S. 213 (1983), satisfying this two-prong test was a strict requirement for establishing probable cause on the basis of information supplied by an informant. In *Gates*, the Supreme Court abandoned the requirement that this two-part test be satisfied and held that the informant's reliability and personal basis of knowledge are simply relevant factors to consider when making a probable cause determination. According to *Gates*, probable cause does not depend on a rigid test. Instead, it involves a common-sense judgment based on the "totality of the circumstances." Although satisfying the two-prong test – informant's reliability and basis of knowledge – is no longer strictly required, it remains an extremely valuable drafting technique.

Usually, it is possible to give some reason why a hearsay source should be believed. If the source is a law enforcement

Probable cause does not depend on a rigid test. Instead, it involves a common-sense judgment based on the "totality of the circumstances."

officer, that is usually enough. If the source is a regular citizen reporting a crime or an eyewitness, the search warrant application should say things like: "This source is simply a concerned good citizen, is not a paid police informer, is gainfully employed, and has no known reason to lie to police."

If the source is a regular police informant, especially if he is a criminal himself, the source's record, if any, of providing accurate information in the past should be recited. If the informant admits participating in the crime, that fact should be included. If the source is paid for accurate information, that should be added.

Corroboration

"Corroboration" is the verification of the accuracy of information received. Corroboration can establish a basis for believing a source of whom little or nothing is known and/or who has no history of providing accurate information. Anything that can be corroborated adds strength to the source's information.

> Corroboration can establish a basis for believing a source of whom little or nothing is known and/or who has no history of providing accurate information.

Even an anonymous tip often can be corroborated by checking out the details provided by the tip. Particularly if the anonymous source can predict accurately future events or provide accurate detailed information that requires insider knowledge, there is reason to accord the tipster heightened credibility.[5] If, however, all an anonymous tipster can do is describe a person who is already in a public place – something anyone can do – and then add a conclusory statement of criminal involvement, that is not enough even to establish reasonable suspicion.[6]

What Is Enough For Probable Cause?

There is no legal formula or scientific test for how much is enough to establish probable cause. Probable cause is ultimately a matter of opinion. As a practical matter, if enough judges agree that the information is sufficient, then there is probable cause. Still, it may help to conceptualize a bit.

Establishing probable cause does not require satisfying a mathematical "more likely than not" standard. In other words, probable cause may not require a 51% likelihood. It requires more than just reasonable suspicion but may be less demanding than the preponderance, or greater weight, of the evidence.[7]

Probable cause admits to the possibility of error. Even at 51% likelihood, the potential for mistake is almost as high as the likelihood of correctness. Probable cause is only a fair probability, not a certainty or proof beyond a reasonable doubt. It is ultimately a common sense judgment made in light of the officer's training and experience and based on the "totality" of the circumstances.

Obtaining The Warrant

When the warrant application form is completed satisfactorily, it may be taken to a neutral, detached judicial official who has authority under state law to issue search warrants. In the presence of that official, the applicant must swear or affirm that the application, often called the "affidavit," is true. If the reviewing official finds the application to be satisfactory, a search warrant (usually on the same form or set of forms) will be issued. Law enforcement officials then must "execute" the warrant.

Search Warrant Execution

While the process of executing a search warrant is partly a matter of state law, certain aspects of the process are fundamental to federal constitutional law. For example, the scope of the search must be based on the probable cause and can be no more expansive or intrusive than the probable cause would permit. Otherwise, the search becomes unreasonable and violates the Fourth Amendment. Federal constitutional law also imposes "knock and announce" requirements and "wait times" before entering.

Following are some questions and considerations that should be part of search warrant execution.

> *The scope of the search must be based on the probable cause and can be no more expansive or intrusive than the probable cause would permit.*

The "Look Right" Test

Does the warrant "look right"? Is the application signed and dated by the applicant and by the issuing judicial official? Does the document contain all its parts? Are all the blocks filled in? Does it look like something is missing? Do the dates make sense? Does the document make sense when you read it? An officer may be held civilly liable for executing an obviously defective warrant.[8]

Jurisdictional Issues

Does the judicial official issuing the warrant have both territorial and subject-matter jurisdiction to issue this warrant? Do the officers who will execute this warrant have both territorial and subject matter jurisdiction to do so? Territorial jurisdiction refers to geographical authority. Where does the official have power to act officially? Subject-matter jurisdiction involves whether or not the official has power to act in a matter of the sort in question.

Time Frames

How long a time frame is allowed to execute this order? Is this order still valid? States typically have laws that a warrant must be executed within a particular period of time following its issuance. So, police may have to begin (or complete) the search within a prescribed period of time under state law. Some states require that certain kinds of warrants be executed only during certain daylight hours.

Re-Check Of Probable Cause

If probable cause has evaporated, the warrant should not be executed but should be returned to the issuing authority for further instructions.

Before a warrant is served, there should be a re-check of probable cause. Has probable cause evaporated? Has the passage of time changed things? Has something new been learned that has caused deterioration of the probable cause? If probable cause has evaporated, the warrant should not be executed but should be returned to the issuing authority for further instructions.

Re-Check Description(s)

The descriptions in the warrant should also be re-checked for accuracy. What is the scope of the authorized search? Care must be taken not to search areas which are not within the probable cause or that are outside the description of places to be searched under the warrant. What are the items to be seized under the warrant? Seizures of items not described in the warrant may sometimes be lawful under the plain view doctrine of warrantless seizure.

Consideration should include any state law rules regarding items seized while executing a search warrant. For example, the old "inadvertence" requirement in the federal plain view doctrine was eliminated by the Supreme Court in *Horton v. California*, 496 U.S. 128 (1990), but it is possible that a state might have retained the inadvertence requirement in its statutory or state constitutional law. Also, a Supreme Court decision, *Arizona v. Hicks*, 480 U.S. 321 (1987), makes clear that to seize an item under the plain view doctrine, one must have probable cause to believe that it is evidence of a crime. It is not enough just to suspect that it is. So, if an item is not listed as an item to be seized in the warrant application, and it is going to be seized, there must be probable cause to believe it is evidence of a crime. That probable cause must exist before the seizure occurs.

Consideration should include any state law rules regarding items seized while executing a search warrant.

Knock And Announce Requirements

The Fourth Amendment and most state laws usually require giving notice of identity and purpose prior to entry. These are commonly referred to as "knock and announce" rules. However, both federal and state law may permit "no knock" entries under certain circumstances. The Fourth Amendment allows a no knock entry if the officer has reasonable suspicion that giving notice would:

1. Endanger someone, or

2. Be futile, or

3. Inhibit effective investigation.[9]

State law regarding no knock entries may be, and often is, more demanding than the federal constitution.

The Fourth Amendment and most state laws usually require giving notice of identity and purpose prior to entry.

Wait Time After Knock And Announce

What is the appropriate "wait time" after the knock and announcement? In some drug cases, a 15- to 20-second wait time is sufficient.[10] A shorter time than that could be enough under some circumstances. The required wait time is not dependent on how long it would take someone to get to the door but rather how long it would take to destroy the evidence sought.

Is There A "Reading" Requirement?

Some state rules require that, after entry, the warrant be read aloud to the person(s) present. In some states, the warrant is read aloud to the premises even if no one except police is present.

"Outside" Assistance

What about "outside" assistance in the execution of the warrant? There are times when a private person could assist dramatically, allowing searches to proceed more quickly, more efficiently, and with less damage. It is best to have specific judicial authorization (in the warrant) if a non-police person is to assist in the search. It is also possible that use of a scent-detection dog could help in searches.

Detaining And Restraining Persons Present During The Execution Of A Warrant

> **Persons present at the scene of a search warrant execution usually may be detained during the search.**

The Supreme Court held in *Michigan v. Summers*, 452 U.S. 692 (1981), that persons present at the scene of a search warrant execution usually may be detained during the search. However, it is possible that, under some circumstances, it would be unreasonable and unconstitutional to detain such persons, even if a state statute would permit the detention. Movement within the premises of persons present may be restricted and/or required as reasonably necessary for the safe and effective conduct of the search.[11]

It is advisable, when possible, to show consideration for personal and/or emotional needs of persons present. In situations where the search is likely to take a great deal of time, special thought should be given to whether or not detention of all persons present is reasonable, and decisions should be made accordingly. In inherently dangerous search warrant executions (involving drug dealers, weapons, etc.), occupants may be restrained in handcuffs.[12]

Protective Sweeps

Consideration should be given to the extent and nature of any "protective sweep" that is likely to be required. A protective sweep is a room-to-room clearance of possible threats. A protective sweep search presents no legal problems unless it extends to areas that would not be searched anyway under the search warrant. These questions should arise, and be resolved, when determining the scope of the search under the warrant. Naturally, officers are permitted to take reasonable protective actions as circumstances arise and shift during the execution of the warrant. Reasonable suspicion is the factual justification requirement for protective sweeps of areas that are not already covered by the search warrant or immediately adjacent to the areas covered.[13]

> **A protective sweep is a room-to-room clearance of possible threats.**

Special Tools And Tactical Teams

The law enforcement agency should also determine to what extent is it appropriate to involve a tactical team in the warrant execution. Would a tactical team be too much for the circumstances? If a tactical team is utilized, is it prepared to engage in transitional tactics – for example, immediately downscaling the tactics – if upon entry, it is learned that they would be unreasonable? What about the use of diversionary devices and distracters like "flash-bangs," etc? Would they create unreasonable dangers under the circumstances or do clear and present risks justify their use? What about gun-pointing, putting people on the floor, and handcuffing? Will those measures likely be reasonable or might they be excessive given the circumstances?

Searches Of Persons Present

What about searching persons present or who arrive at private premises during the execution of the warrant? A Supreme

> **Persons in a public area may not be automatically frisked just because police are executing a search warrant in the premises.**

Court decision, *Ybarra v. Illinois*, 444 U.S. 85 (1979), holds that persons in a public area (a bar, in that case) may not be automatically frisked just because police are executing a search warrant in the premises. Instead, officers must adhere to normal legal requirements for non-consensual frisks – reasonable suspicion of the presence of weapons.

It is advisable to follow the same rule in private premises searches, even though some states have statutory law that purports to allow essentially automatic frisks in such cases. The general rule is that persons present on private premises are not necessarily subject to frisk and/or full search just because they are on the premises where a search warrant is executed. Any such searches must be carefully conformed to the reasonableness requirement of the Fourth Amendment, even if state statutory law purports to authorize "automatic" searches. Upon entering the premises, a full search of persons present may be conducted if the persons are described as "places" to be searched under the warrant or if there is already probable cause to arrest those persons. In other situations, it is sometimes advisable to postpone the decision as to full search of persons present until the premises search is complete. At that time, it may be easier to determine whether or not there is probable cause to search and/or arrest the persons present and a better decision can be made.

NOTE: The term "full search" used in the above paragraph means the kind of search typically conducted by an officer in a thorough search incident to arrest. It would not usually include strip searches, complete or partial, and would definitely not include body cavity searches except under the most compelling exigent circumstances. Body cavity probes should be conducted only by certified medical personnel.

> **The Fourth Amendment prohibits taking or allowing news media representatives into private premises with a search team.**

Media Involvement

In 1999, the Supreme Court decided in two cases that the Fourth Amendment prohibits taking or allowing news media representatives into private premises with a search team. This method of creating publicity is now clearly unconstitutional.[14] Of course, these holdings do not eliminate the possibility of a voluntary consent from residents/occupants to the media intrusion. In seeking such a consent, police would have to communicate with the residents/occupants very carefully in order to avoid coerciveness that could otherwise be present in such a transaction.

Length Of Search

The warrant-based search should be terminated when all items subject to seizure under the warrant have been located or when it has become apparent that a search of reasonable scope and duration will not disclose the items to be seized. In some cases, it may be necessary and/or desirable to seek the issuance of a second warrant so that additional search action may be lawfully conducted.

Securing The Premises

When leaving the search scene, particularly one that is or will be unoccupied because of arrests, reasonable steps should be taken to assure that the premises are protected and/or secured. This may sometimes require providing police protection of the premises until repairs can be made or other security measures can be arranged and completed.

Care Of Evidence

Great care should be taken to assure that items seized during the search are protected and accounted for through a strict chain of custody. State law and agency policy should be reviewed to assure compliance with inventory and receipt requirements.

"Return" Of Warrant

Most states and some local jurisdictions have prescribed procedures for the "return" of the warrant, whether or not the warrant is executed and property seized, to the judicial authorities that issued the warrant. Officers should take care to follow applicable state law and/or local procedural rules.

After-Action Reports

Although not usually a legal requirement, a thorough documentation of the activities surrounding search warrant execution is a good idea, both to minimize liability exposure and to further other organizational work – policy making, training, etc.

NOTES

[1] See *Massachusetts v. Sheppard*, 468 U.S. 981 (1984) and *United States v. Leon*, 468 U.S. 897 (1984).

[2] See, for example, *United States v. Grubbs*, 547 U.S. 90 (2006).

[3] See, for example, *United States v. Hang Le-Thy Tran*, 433 F.3d 472 (6th Cir. 2006).

[4] *United States v. Tamari*, 454 F.3d 1259 (11th Cir. 2006). See *United States v. Angelos*, 433 F.3d 738 (10th Cir. 2006) for an example of exceeding the description of the place to be searched.

[5] See, as examples, *Alabama v. White*, 496 U.S. 325 (1990) and *Illinois v. Gates*, 462 U.S. 213 (1983).

[6] See, for example, *Florida v. J. L.*, 529 U.S. 266 (2000).

[7] See *Maryland v. Pringle*, 540 U.S. 366 (2003), in which the Court stated that the preponderance of the evidence standard "has no place" in a probable cause determination.

[8] *Groh v. Ramirez*, 540 U.S. 551 (2004).

[9] See *Richards v. Wisconsin*, 520 U.S. 385 (1997); *Wilson v. Arkansas*, 514 U.S. 927 (1995); and *Hudson v. Michigan*, 547 U.S. 586 (2006).

[10] See *United States v. Banks*, 540 U.S. 31 (2003).

[11] See, for example, *Illinois v. McArthur*, 531 U.S. 326 (2001).

[12] *Muehler v. Mena*, 544 U.S. 93 (2005).

[13] See *Maryland v. Buie*, 494 U.S. 325 (1990).

[14] See *Hanlon v. Berger*, 526 U.S. 808 (1999) and *Wilson v. Layne*, 526 U.S. 603 (1999).

CHAPTER 13

NON-TESTIMONIAL IDENTIFICATION PROCEDURES

The Fifth Amendment protects people from being compelled to give <u>testimonial</u> evidence against themselves in a criminal proceeding. Non-testimonial identification evidence such as fingerprints, handwriting samples and body fluids, may be taken from suspects under certain circumstances without violating Fifth Amendment rights, but may still involve Fourth Amendment rights. This discussion helps answer three questions:

1. What are non-testimonial identification procedures?

2. Which of these procedures are permissible incident to arrest and/or custody?

3. How, if at all, may lawful non-testimonial identification procedures be accomplished out of custody?

What Are Non-Testimonial Identification Procedures?

As the name indicates, non-testimonial identification procedures involve identification evidence other than a subject's own testimony. The retrieval of non-testimonial identification evidence from criminal suspects is vitally important to the successful resolution of many criminal investigations. Oftentimes, a thorough processing of a crime scene and/or victim's body will yield fingerprints, palm prints, footprints, hair, or body fluid evidence. These evidentiary items may be compared later with samples obtained from suspects.

In some investigative scenarios where there are eyewitnesses to a crime, a lineup involving the suspect may be arranged. In other situations, a suspect's voice may be compared by witnesses to the remembered sound of a perpetrator's voice. A suspect's handwriting may be compared, in some cases, to evidentiary documents containing the perpetrator's handwriting.

The use by police of non-testimonial identification procedures may involve a variety of legal rights which could protect a suspect and create issues for the investigating officer. The violation of a suspect's rights in non-testimonial identification procedures can create civil liability exposure for officers and agencies

The use by police of non-testimonial identification procedures may involve a variety of legal rights which could protect a suspect and create issues for the investigating officer.

and can cause the suppression or exclusion of resulting derivative evidence. These rights could include:

State law rights. Note that state law may be more restrictive/demanding than the federal constitution. Often this is particularly so in the case of juvenile suspects.

Fourth Amendment search and seizure rights. If non-testimonial identification evidence is derived from an illegal detention, arrest, search, or use of force, the evidence may be excluded from trial consideration.[1] Obviously, civil liability exposure is also present in such circumstances.

Sixth Amendment right to counsel after formal charging. Certain non-testimonial identification procedures require involvement of a defendant's lawyer, if they occur after formal charging (indictment or arraignment) and if the defendant does not waive the right.[2]

Fourteenth Amendment due process rights. Due process of law includes the concept of "fundamental fairness." This would require, for example, that a lineup identification process not be unduly "suggestive" of any particular suspect, i.e., that it be "fair."

Since the retrieval of non-testimonial evidence from suspects does not involve compelled testimony, the Fifth Amendment prohibition against compelled self-incrimination is not implicated by non-testimonial identification procedures. If a person were to voluntarily consent to a non-testimonial identification procedure, the procedure would not implicate the Fourth Amendment.

Non-Testimonial Evidence Gained Through A Search Incident To An Arrest

A lawful, custodial arrest carries with it the authority to retrieve, in a search incident to that arrest, certain non-testimonial evidentiary items from the person of the arrestee.

A lawful, custodial arrest carries with it the authority to retrieve, in a search incident to that arrest, certain non-testimonial evidentiary items from the person of the arrestee.[3] This non-testimonial evidence may include lineup identification, fingerprints, palm prints, footprints, photographs, body measurements, head hair samples, fingernail scrapings, and gunshot residue, and in arrests for serious offenses, DNA buccal swabs.[4] If a person under arrest resists these processes, reasonable force may be utilized to overcome the resistance and recover the desired non-testimonial evidence. Typically, this force would involve utilizing several officers and/or special equipment such as restraints to reduce or eliminate risk of injury to the arrestee. Ideally, it would also involve a court order directing the use of that force reasonably necessary to accomplish the procedure.

Body Searches

Significant bodily intrusions (nonconsensual withdrawal of blood, stomach pumping, and surgical procedures, as examples) typically require a search warrant or similar court order. Occasionally, exigent circumstances may excuse the warrant requirement, such as where there is an immediate need to gather evidence of rapidly changing blood alcohol content of a drunk driver after an accident involving serious injuries or fatalities.[5] However, in *Missouri v. McNeely*, 133 S. Ct. 1552 (2013), the Supreme Court held that this exigent circumstance does not exist in "routine" drunk driving cases.

Significant bodily intrusions typically require a search warrant or similar court order.

Non-Testimonial Identification Orders

A much different situation exists when police do not have probable cause to arrest, but wish to obtain non-testimonial evidence from a subject. It appears that the federal constitution and many state laws permit a court-ordered requirement that a person submit to non-testimonial identification procedures based upon a government showing of reasonable suspicion. In some states that court order is called a "non-testimonial identification order." Even if there is not a statutory procedure in a particular state, a judge or other judicial official could have inherent common law judicial power to issue an order "in the interest of justice" that would permit such a procedure. Such a procedure involves a requirement that a suspect briefly present himself to police or medical personnel for the limited purpose of collecting physical evidence from that person or participating in an identification process.

Usually, states have two criteria built into their statutory procedures for the issuance of a non-testimonial identification order:

1. Probable cause to believe that a crime has been committed; plus

2. Reasonable suspicion that the person from whom the government seeks to retrieve non-testimonial evidence committed the crime.

Naturally, there also must be reason to believe the identification process would be useful, given existing evidence, in identifying the perpetrator.

An officer seeking a non-testimonial identification order typically must construct a "reasonable suspicion statement" using the same principles as in drafting a probable cause statement in a search warrant application. The principal difference is that only reasonable suspicion must be demonstrated. Of course, if probable cause were already present, officers could use a search warrant for non-testimonial identification procedures or in some cases simply make an arrest and conduct a search incident to arrest.

Service Or Execution Of Non-Testimonial Identification Orders

Because only reasonable suspicion of a person's involvement in a crime has been shown, execution of non-testimonial identification orders differs dramatically from the execution of an arrest warrant. Service of a non-testimonial identification order typically does not involve taking the subject into custody. Instead, it consists only of delivering the court papers and notifying the suspect that he/she must appear at a specific place, usually police or medical facilities, within or at a specified time. The non-testimonial identification order specifies what non-testimonial evidence and/or procedures will be retrieved or conducted. In most states that allow such procedures, a suspect's failure to obey the non-testimonial identification order is contempt of court.

Service of a non-testimonial identification order typically does not involve taking the subject into custody.

Consent Or Search Warrants

Obtaining a person's consent to the recovery of non-testimonial identification evidence is always an option in lieu of seeking a court order. Seeking a search warrant for the retrieval of non-testimonial identification evidence is also an option if probable cause exists. In such cases, probable cause often would also exist to arrest the suspect for the crime and some non-testimonial evidence might be recovered without a search warrant in a search incident to the custodial arrest.

Juveniles

There are often additional state statutory provisions governing non-testimonial identification procedures involving juveniles. Such statutes are usually more restrictive of police procedure than is federal constitutional law. It is possible that even consensual recovery of non-testimonial identification evidence like fingerprints may be restricted or prohibited under state law regarding juveniles.

Lineups And Photographic Arrays

Lineups involve displaying a suspect's person and/or photograph, along with those of others, to a victim or witness for possible identification of the perpetrator. Lineups come in two varieties: Physical lineups involving actual people (sometimes called "corporal" or "body" lineups and today seldom used) and photographic lineups or "arrays." Everyone knows how easily eyewitness identification processes can go awry and there is not much worse that can happen in police work than sending an innocent person to prison. Accordingly, there are a variety of methods that can be used to improve reliability and reduce suggestiveness in these procedures.

There is no constitutional requirement that a body lineup or photographic array contain a certain number of participants or photos. Rather, the requirement is simply that the procedure be "fair" – that is, not unduly suggestive. Generally, five or six photographs or persons is adequate. Smaller numbers usually increase the suggestiveness of the array and create consequent problems.

There is no constitutional requirement that a body lineup or photographic array contain a certain number of participants or photos.

There are several fundamental principles that reduce suggestiveness in both photographic and physical lineups. The witness or victim should be informed that the perpetrator may or may not be in the lineup and that the witness or victim is under no obligation to identify anyone. Photographs should be presented to the witness sequentially, not as a single display of multiple photographs, and, unless it is impossible to do so, should involve many more photos than just five or six. The witness or victim should not be informed that he or she has identified the "right" person. Witnesses should not be allowed to collaborate and should view the lineups separately and individually. There is value is asking the witness for a "confidence statement" expressing as a percentage or phrase the degree of confidence that the witness has in the identification. Using an uninvolved officer who does not know who the suspect is reduces potentials for nuanced behavior creating suggestiveness.

> **The people appearing in the lineup or array should have a similar appearance to the suspect, typically sharing physical characteristics such as gender, race, age, and facial hair.**

Of course, the people appearing in the lineup or array should have a similar appearance to the suspect, typically sharing physical characteristics such as gender, race, age, and facial hair. Care should be taken to ensure there are no distinguishing features that draw attention to the suspect over the other choices. Physical lineups are difficult to accomplish and are rarely necessary. Photographic arrays are preferable because they are usually much easier to produce and can be easily preserved for trial review.

Scenario #79 A police officer is preparing a photo array to further a robbery investigation. According to the victim-eyewitness, the perpetrator was an Hispanic male with a tattoo on his forehead and a person of that description has now been arrested. This photo array consists of five people: 1) a black male with a tattoo on his forehead; 2) an Asian male with a tattoo on his forehead; 3) a white male with a tattoo on his forehead; 4) the suspect that has been arrested; and 5) an Hispanic male with no tattoo on his forehead.

Question: Is this a fair and lawful photo array?

> Answer: No. This photo array is unduly suggestive because the only picture of a person matching the witness' description is the suspect. All of the photos should be of Hispanic males with tattoos on their foreheads, which illustrates one of several reasons why photo arrays are preferable to body lineups – photo arrays are easier to produce.

When Does The Right To Counsel Attach During The Identification Process?

The Sixth Amendment right to counsel "attaches" upon formal charging. After formal charging has occurred, the suspect has a right to counsel at all critical stages of adversary judicial proceedings. A suspect's participation in a physical lineup is considered a "critical stage."[6] The conduct of a photographic lineup or array is not.[7]

In many states, formal charging is called "arraignment" or "first appearance." Formal charging is generally marked by the first time the defendant appears in court before a judge and prosecutor. The person usually is informed of the charges against him, asked how he pleads, and an inquiry is made concerning appointment of counsel. This signals the initiation of adversary judicial proceedings – the State has committed its resources to prosecute the suspect. Formal charging also has occurred if there has been a grand jury indictment.

The suspect's right to counsel at a physical lineup conducted after formal charging may be waived.[8] To obtain a waiver, the officer should explain the following to the suspect:

1. He will be placed in a lineup with several other people.

2. A witness will view this lineup in an attempt to identify the perpetrator of a crime.

3. In respect to this lineup he has a right to have a lawyer present to observe the lineup and to advise him.

4. If he cannot afford a lawyer and wants one, one will be appointed to represent him during the lineup.

The suspect's right to counsel at a physical lineup conducted after formal charging may be waived.

The officer may then solicit a waiver of rights:

"Do you understand the rights I have explained to you?"

"Do you wish to have an attorney represent you during this lineup?"

Though the right to counsel does not exist prior to formal charging, the presence of the suspect's attorney may quiet later allegations of unfairness and due process violations.

For practical reasons, officers should consider having a lawyer present at lineups even when there have not yet been formal charges. Though the right to counsel does not exist prior to formal charging, the presence of the suspect's attorney may quiet later allegations of unfairness and due process violations.

NOTE: As mentioned, the Sixth Amendment right to counsel applies only to formally-charged matters. If a person has been formally charged in one matter, but a lineup involves a different offense, there usually would be no Sixth Amendment right to counsel in a lineup involving the uncharged matter.

Impermissible Suggestiveness In A Lineup Or Photo Array

An impermissibly suggestive identification procedure may violate the Fourteenth Amendment due process clause, thus creating liability exposures and problems with later in-court identification. Whether the suggestiveness of a procedure is impermissible is judged by a "totality of circumstances" test.[9] If the identification procedure is unconstitutionally suggestive, the Court will examine the following factors in deciding whether or not to allow an in-court identification:

1. The quality and length of the original viewing (i.e., at the crime) of the suspect by the eyewitness.

2. The degree of attention shown by the eyewitness at the original viewing.

3. The accuracy of the prior description given by the eyewitness.

4. The percentage of certainty in the identification procedure.

5. The length of time between the crime and the identification procedure.[10]

The key question the Court will decide is whether the tainted identification procedure created a substantial risk of misidentification in court. If the answer is "yes," in-court identification would not be permitted. It is quite possible that the answer may be "no," given analysis of the above factor, and that in-court identification may be allowed notwithstanding the impropriety of the earlier identification process.

> *The key question the Court will decide is whether the tainted identification procedure created a substantial risk of misidentification in court.*

Show-Ups

A show-up is display of just one person or photograph to an eyewitness. The witness is simply asked, "Do you recognize this person?" Show-ups should be used very carefully and only soon after a crime occurs, within a few hours, usually. Such procedures, though obviously suggestive, have been approved by the courts because:

1. The victim/witness memory is the best it will ever be.

2. There is a strong need to determine if a detained person is in fact the perpetrator.

3. The suspect is not as likely to have altered his appearance as he might later, and an appropriate identification may be facilitated.

4. If it is determined that a wrong person has been detained, then that person may be quickly released and search for the actual perpetrator may be swiftly resumed.

As put by the Eighth Circuit Court of Appeals in *United States v. King*, 148 F.3d 968 (8th Cir. 1998),"quick, on-the-scene identification" is "essential to free innocent suspects and to inform police if further investigation is necessary."[11] Suggestiveness may be reduced somewhat by advising the victim/witness that the subject to be viewed "may or may not" be the perpetrator. A recent case holds that removal or manipulation of a suspect's clothing (e.g., taking off a jacket to display his shirt) to make him look more like the described perpetrator is not impermissible during an investigative detention show-up.[12]

Uncooperativeness

If a person subject to a valid non-testimonial identification court order refuses to cooperate with the procedure, several possibilities exist:

1. The court issuing the order could hold the subject in contempt of court and attempt thereby to force his cooperation.

2. The prosecutor may be able to comment and/or produce evidence in court that the subject was uncooperative, raising the inference of the suspect's guilt.

3. If, given its nature, the identification procedure could be appropriately accomplished by force, a court could order that necessary force be used. If a person who is in custody refuses to submit to a procedure which reasonably could be completed forcibly, police may use limited force as reasonably necessary to accomplish the procedure. If it is a body lineup that is refused, police may resort to a photo array. Some have suggested that refusal to participate in a lineup could make a show-up necessary. In such a conflicted situation, obtaining legal advice and/or judicial guidance would be wise.

> *If a person who is in custody refuses to submit to a procedure which reasonably could be completed forcibly, police may use limited force as reasonably necessary to accomplish the procedure.*

NOTES

[1] See *Hayes v. Florida*, 470 U.S. 811 (1985), for example.

[2] *Kirby v. Illinois*, 406 U.S. 682 (1972) and *United States v. Wade*, 388 U.S. 218 (1967).

[3] See *Cupp v. Murphy*, 412 U.S. 291 (1973).

[4] See *Maryland v. King*, 133 S. Ct. 1958 (2013).

[5] See, for example, *Schmerber v. California*, 384 U.S. 757 (1966). See also *Winston v. Lee*, 470 U.S. 753 (1985), which involved a minor surgical intrusion to recover a bullet.

[6] *Kirby v. Illinois*, 406 U.S. 682 (1972).

[7] See *United States v. Ash*, 413 U.S. 300 (1973).

[8] *United States v. Wade*, 388 U.S. 218 (1967).

[9] See *Stovall v. Denno*, 388 U.S. 293 (1967); *Simmons v. United States*, 390 U.S. 377 (1968); *Neil v. Biggers*, 409 U.S. 188 (1972); and *Manson v. Brathwaite*, 432 U.S. 98 (1977).

[10] See *Manson v. Brathwaite*, 432 U.S. 98 (1977).

[11] See also *United States v. Pickar*, 616 F.3d 821 (8th Cir. 2010).

[12] *United States v. Askew*, 482 F.3d 532 (D.C. Cir. 2007).

CHAPTER 14

THE USE OF FORCE IN POLICE PROCEDURES

The Fourth Amendment Standard Of "Objective Reasonableness"

In *Graham v. Connor*, 490 U.S. 386 (1989), the Supreme Court held that police use of force to seize people who are not already jailed or imprisoned should be analyzed under the Fourth Amendment's "objective reasonableness" standard. Before *Graham*, two leading cases guided use of force analysis and both used "subjective" tests. In *Rochin v. California*, 342 U.S. 165 (1952), the Court concerned itself with behavior that "shocks the conscience." In *Johnson v. Glick*, 481 F.2d 1028 (2d Cir. 1973), the focus was whether the force was applied in a good faith effort to maintain order or sadistically and with malice for the very purpose of causing harm. These cases created tests which turned on the involved officer's state of mind and heart and/or the sensibilities of a particular judge or jury.

Graham erased these comparatively subjective standards and replaced them with one which does not involve subjective inquiries into the law enforcement officer's thoughts, feelings, and motivations. Instead, *Graham* requires examination of only objective circumstances and a "reasonable" officer's response to them.

The *Graham* case began on November 12, 1984, when Dethorne Graham was driven by a friend, William Berry, to a convenience store near Graham's home. Graham quickly entered the store, but immediately left again in a hurried manner. Graham got back into the car with Berry, who quickly drove away. M.S. Connor, a Charlotte police officer, saw all of this. His suspicions aroused, he followed Berry and Graham in his patrol car. Approximately one-half mile from the convenience store, Officer Connor stopped the car containing Berry and Graham to determine what, if anything, had happened at the convenience store.

When Connor approached the car, Berry told Connor that Graham was simply having a "sugar reaction." Connor directed them to wait. After Connor told him he had to wait, Graham got out of Berry's car, running around it twice. Berry asked for Connor's help and, together, they caught Graham and held him,

> **Police use of force to seize people who are not already jailed or imprisoned should be analyzed under the Fourth Amendment's "objective reasonableness" standard.**

though he was still struggling. In the meantime, four other uniformed Charlotte police officers arrived in response to Officer Connor's request for assistance. They struggled with Graham, before eventually handcuffing him and placing him in a police car. When Officer Connor learned that Graham had committed no crime in the convenience store, police took Graham home and released him. At some point during this contact with police, Graham broke his foot, received cuts on the wrists, bruises on his forehead, and a shoulder injury. He also claimed to have developed a loud ringing in his ear. As bad luck would have it, he was indeed an insulin-dependent diabetic suffering an insulin reaction.

Graham sued the five officers and the City of Charlotte for perceived constitutional rights violations, alleging excessive force in the investigatory stop. The case was tried before a jury. At the close of Graham's case, the trial court directed verdicts for the defendants, using a partly subjective test (pursuant to *Johnson v. Glick*) and finding no evidence of malice or bad faith. An appeal by plaintiff to the United States Court of Appeals for the Fourth Circuit was unsuccessful. Graham then appealed to the Supreme Court, which found that the lower courts had applied an incorrect standard, then set a new one, referring initially to its four-year-old deadly force decision in *Tennessee v. Garner*, 471 U.S. 1 (1985):

> "Today we make explicit what was implicit in *Garner's* analysis, and hold that all claims that law enforcement officers have used excessive force – deadly or not – in the course of an arrest, investigatory stop, or other 'seizure' of a free citizen should be analyzed under the Fourth Amendment and its 'reasonableness' standard, rather than under a 'substantive due process' approach...
>
> "Legal analysis in this area requires careful attention to the facts and circumstances of each particular case, including the severity of the crime at issue, whether the suspect poses an immediate threat to the safety of the officers or others, and whether he is actively resisting arrest or attempting to evade arrest by flight."

Adding to the picture, the *Graham* Court continued: "The 'reasonableness' of a particular use of force must be judged from the perspective of a reasonable officer on the scene, rather than with the 20/20 vision of hindsight." Noting that other areas of Fourth Amendment law allow an officer leeway for imperfect decision making, especially given the difficulties of police work, the Court then observed, quoting in part from *Johnson v. Glick*:

> "…with respect to a claim of excessive force, the same standard of reasonableness at the moment applies: 'Not every push or shove, even if it may later seem unnecessary in the peace of a judge's chambers,' violates the Fourth Amendment. The calculus of reasonableness must embody allowance for the fact that police officers are often forced to make split-second judgments – in circumstances that are tense, uncertain, and rapidly evolving – about the amount of force that is necessary in a particular situation.
>
> "As in other Fourth Amendment contexts, however, the 'reasonableness' inquiry in an excessive force case is an objective one: The question is whether the officers' actions are 'objectively reasonable' in light of the facts and circumstances confronting them, without regard to their underlying intent or motivation. An officer's evil intentions will not make a Fourth Amendment violation out of an objectively reasonable use of force; nor will an officer's good intentions make an objectively unreasonable use of force constitutional…The Fourth Amendment inquiry is one of 'objective reasonableness' under the circumstances, and subjective concepts like 'malice' and 'sadism' have no proper place in that inquiry."

Reasonableness must embody allowance for the fact that police officers are often forced to make split-second judgments.

Because the District Court and the Court of Appeals erroneously applied a subjective standard, the case was sent back for reconsideration under the newly-prescribed Fourth Amendment standard of objective reasonableness. In the ensuing new trial using the objective standard, police defendants again won, this time in a jury verdict in their favor.

The standard arising from *Graham* is entirely objective – could a reasonable, well-trained officer think it necessary to use a like amount of force under like circumstances? If the answer is "yes," the force is reasonable and therefore constitutional.

Deadly Force

In *Tennessee v. Garner*, 471 U.S. 1 (1985), the Supreme Court established a federal constitutional standard for police use of deadly force to prevent the escape of suspected criminals. The language of the Court's opinion also shed some light on the issue of deadly force used by police in self-defense. According to the Supreme Court, the facts of *Tennessee v. Garner* were as follows.

At about 10:45 p.m. on October 3, 1974, two Memphis police officers, Hymon and Wright, were dispatched to answer a "prowler inside" call. Upon arriving at the scene they saw a woman standing on her porch and gesturing toward the adjacent house. She told them she had heard glass breaking and that "they" or "someone" was breaking in next door. While Wright radioed the dispatcher to say that they were on the scene, Hymon went behind the house. He heard a door slam and saw someone run across the backyard. The fleeing suspect, Edward Garner, stopped at a six-foot-high chain link fence at the edge of the yard. With the aid of a flashlight, Hymon was able to see Garner's face and hands. He saw no sign of a weapon and, though not certain, was "reasonably sure" that Garner was unarmed. He also thought Garner was 17 or 18 years old and 5'5" or 5'7" tall. (In fact, Garner turned out to be a 15-year-old eighth grader, 5'4", about 100 to 110 pounds.) While Garner was crouched at the base of the fence, Hymon called out "Police, Halt!" and took a few steps toward him. Garner then began to climb over the fence. Convinced that if Garner made it over the fence he would escape, Hymon shot him. Garner was taken by ambulance to a hospital, where he died on the operating table. Ten dollars and a purse taken from the house were found with him.

In using deadly force to prevent the escape, Hymon was acting under authority of a Tennessee statute and pursuant to Police

> **The Supreme Court established a federal constitutional standard for police use of deadly force to prevent the escape of suspected criminals.**

Department policy, both of which allowed deadly force to prevent escape of at least some felony suspects. The Memphis Police Department's policy was slightly more restrictive than the statute, but still allowed the use of deadly force in cases of burglary. The incident was reviewed by the Memphis Police Firearm's Review Board and presented to a grand jury. Neither took action against Officer Hymon.

When asked at trial why he fired, Hymon basically explained in detail why, had he not fired, the suspect likely would have gotten away. While today many would scoff at such a limited rationale, at the time of the incident much police policy and training embraced state statutory law which in turn reflected the common law "fleeing felon rule" – all of which allowed use of deadly force in such circumstances. The Supreme Court decided to step in.

The issue in the case, according to the Supreme Court, was "the constitutionality of the use of deadly force to prevent the escape of an apparently unarmed suspected felon." The Court held that "such force may not be used unless it is necessary to prevent the escape and the officer has probable cause to believe that the suspect poses a significant threat of death or serious physical injury to the officer or others." As put by the Court:

> "The use of deadly force to prevent the escape of all felony suspects, whatever the circumstances, is constitutionally unreasonable. It is not better that all felony suspects die than that they escape. Where the suspect poses no immediate threat to the officer and no threat to others, the harm resulting from failing to apprehend him does not justify the use of deadly force to do so. It is no doubt unfortunate when a suspect who is in sight escapes, but the fact that the police arrive a little late or are a little slower afoot does not always justify killing the suspect. A police officer may not seize an unarmed, nondangerous suspect by shooting him dead…
>
> "Where the officer has probable cause to believe…that the suspect poses a threat of serious physical harm, either to the officer or to others, it is not constitutionally unreasonable to prevent escapes

It is not better that all felony suspects die than that they escape.

by using deadly force. Thus, if the suspect threatens the officer with a weapon or there is probable cause to believe that he has committed a crime involving the infliction or threatened infliction of serious physical harm, deadly force may be used if necessary to prevent escape, and if, where feasible, some warning has been given."

An analysis of the *Garner* opinion is aided by breaking down the immediately preceding paragraph into its subparts:

1. Life-threatening Escape. "Where the officer has probable cause to believe that the suspect poses a threat of serious physical harm, either to the officer or others, it is not constitutionally unreasonable to prevent escape by using deadly force." This language focuses on the manner of escape and the threat posed by that escape. If the manner of the escape itself creates an imminent threat of death or serious physical harm to the officer or others, the Fourth Amendment permits deadly force to prevent the escape – without regard to the type of crime originally committed.[1]

2. Life-Threatening Felony. "…if the suspect threatens the officer with a weapon or there is probable cause to believe that he has committed a crime involving the infliction or threatened infliction of serious physical harm, deadly force may be used if necessary to prevent escape, and if, where feasible, some warning has been given." (emphasis added) Here, the language after the disjunctive "or" focuses not on the manner of escape but on the nature of the crime which the suspect has apparently committed. It appears from this language that the Fourth Amendment permits deadly force to prevent escape of certain criminals, even if they are unarmed and non-threatening at the time of their escape efforts.[2]

3. Some Warning Where Feasible. In the clause analyzed immediately above, the Supreme Court created a constitutional requirement that "some warning" be given prior to the use of deadly force "where feasible." Because many states do not have such a requirement under their statutes or court decisions, this federal "warning" requirement is an important addition to the law. The absence of this warning, if it was feasible to give it, could make an otherwise constitutional shooting unconstitu-

> *The Supreme Court created a constitutional requirement that "some warning" be given prior to the use of deadly force "where feasible."*

tional. Presumably, the warning referred to is in the nature of "Police! Stop or I'll shoot!"

4. If Necessary To Prevent Escape. These words impose what is known as the "reasonable necessity" rule. In order for deadly force to be constitutionally permissible, there must be probable cause to believe that the use of deadly force is "reasonably necessary" – that if deadly force is not employed, the escape will probably succeed. In some cases, reasonable necessity will mean that foot pursuit plus non-deadly force would not likely result in apprehension. In other cases, it will mean that delay in apprehension would create substantial and unreasonable risk to the police or others of death or serious physical injury.

> In order for deadly force to be constitutionally permissible, there must be probable cause to believe that the use of deadly force is "reasonably necessary."

What manner of escape activity will permit deadly force under the constitutional standard? What types of crimes will, in and of themselves, justify the use of deadly force to prevent escape of the perpetrator? Certainly the use or threatened use of a deadly weapon by the suspect in his escape effort creates constitutional authority to use deadly force to prevent the escape. Hostage-taking and/or life threatening attacks during escape efforts, even by unarmed suspects, would likely permit deadly force. Crimes which would seem to qualify as involving the infliction or threatened infliction of serious physical harm include homicides, armed robberies, and life-threatening felonious assaults, as well as certain forms of kidnapping, arson, and rape. Although the *Garner* case does not make it clear, caution dictates that its rule regarding deadly force to apprehend these certain types of criminals probably should be applied only during the suspect's immediate and continuous flight from the crime scene or area. The use of deadly force to prevent his escape when spotted two weeks or two hours after the crime is highly questionable, at best.

Federal constitutional law permits law enforcement officers to use deadly force to apprehend criminal suspects when there is "probable cause to believe that the suspect poses a threat of serious physical harm…to the officer or to others…" and if deadly force "is necessary" to effect the apprehensions. So two factors – dangerousness and necessity – are relevant to the question whether deadly force is constitutionally permissible.

> Federal constitutional law permits law enforcement officers to use deadly force to apprehend criminal suspects when there is "probable cause to believe that the suspect poses a threat of serious physical harm…to the officer or to others…"

NOTE: Some state law and many police department policies are considerably more restrictive of deadly force than is the federal constitutional standard.

No Requirement Of Least Intrusive Alternative

Because the *Graham v. Connor* use of force standard has been so helpful to police in civil lawsuits, attorneys representing plaintiffs often challenge officer decision making on peripheral and preceding matters in an effort to make them the focus of constitutional concern. Such claims include:

1. Less intrusive alternatives were available and should have been used; therefore, the force actually used was not reasonable; or

2. The officer made choices and took actions that were not necessary, thereby creating the necessity for the use of force.

An officer is not required by the Constitution to use the least intrusive force alternative, only a "reasonable" one.

Fortunately for police, federal appeals courts have established a clearly discernible trend that an officer is not required by the Constitution to use the least intrusive force alternative, only a "reasonable" one. Also, the fact an officer could have made better choices or decisions in the events that preceded the application of force will not render the officer's force response unconstitutional.

In *Cole v. Bone*, 993 F.2d 1328 (8th Cir. 1993), the Eighth Circuit United States Court of Appeals stated: "The Constitution...requires only that the seizure be objectively reasonable, not that the officer pursue the most prudent course of action as judged by 20/20 hindsight." In *Illinois v. Lafayette*, 462 U.S. 640 (1983), an inventory search case, the Supreme Court held that the Fourth Amendment does not require selection of "the least intrusive alternative, only a reasonable one." In *Plakas v. Drinski*, 19 F.3d 1143 (7th Cir. 1994), plaintiffs argued that the officer should have used non-deadly alternatives, such as chemical mace or a canine, to defeat the threat caused by a handcuffed but fireplace poker wielding assailant. The federal Seventh Circuit Court of Appeals rejected the argument:

> "There is no precedent in this Circuit (or any other) which says that the Constitution requires police to use all feasible alternatives to avoid a situation where deadly force can justifiably be used. There are, however, cases which support the assertion that where deadly force is otherwise justified under the Constitution, there is no constitutional duty to use non-deadly alternatives first.
>
> "As [the suspect] moved toward [the officer], was he supposed to think of an attack dog, of...CS gas, of how fast he could run backward? Our answer is, and has been, no, because there is too little time for the officer to do so and too much opportunity to second-guess that officer."

Responding directly to the plaintiff's contention that police should have had and used non-deadly or "less-lethal" force equipment, the Court ruled:

> "There can be reasonable debates about whether the Constitution also enacts a code of criminal procedure, but we think it is clear that the Constitution does not enact a police administrator's equipment list."

Then rejecting the argument that the officer was constitutionally-required to have acted differently in the events preceding the use of force, the Court found that such analysis would "nearly always reveal that something different could have been done if the officer knew the future before it occurred..." and stated:

> "Other than random attacks, all such cases begin with the decision of a police officer to do something, to help, to arrest, to inquire. If the officer had decided to do nothing, then no force would have been used. In this sense, the police officer always causes the trouble. However, it is trouble which the police officer is sworn to cause, which society pays him to cause and which, if kept within constitutional limits, society praises the officer for causing."

Likewise in *Scott v. Henrich*, 39 F.3d 912 (9th Cir. 1994), the plaintiff claimed that the officers should have proceeded differently and thereby might have avoided the need for deadly force. The Appellate Court rejected plaintiff's argument and had this to say:

> "Requiring officers to find and choose the least intrusive alternative would require them to exercise superhuman judgment. In the heat of battle with lives potentially in the balance, an officer would not be able to rely on training and common sense to decide what would best accomplish his mission. Instead, he would need to ascertain the least intrusive alternative (an inherently subjective determination) and choose that option and that option only. Imposing such a requirement would inevitably induce tentativeness by officers, and thus deter police from protecting the public and themselves. It would also entangle the courts in endless second-guessing of police decisions made under stress and subject to the exigencies of the moment."

> *"Requiring officers to find and choose the least intrusive alternative would require them to exercise superhuman judgment."*

A more recent adoption of these principles is found in *Scott v. Edinburg*, 346 F.3d 752 (7th Cir. 2003). In that case, the Court noted that federal law protects plaintiffs from constitutional violations, not violations of state law, departmental regulations, or best practices. Another example of this line of decision-making is *Carter v. Buscher*, 973 F.2d 1328 (7th Cir. 1992). In that case, police created a plan to arrest a man who had contracted to have his wife killed. When the plan was executed, the suspect was able to shoot and kill one officer and wound another before being killed himself. Ironically (in the extreme), the deceased suspect's wife who was the intended victim of her husband's contract murder plan then sued police, alleging that they should have planned differently and better, and thus would not have provoked her husband into firing on police and getting himself shot. The reviewing appeals court first found that "pre-seizure conduct is not subject to Fourth Amendment scrutiny," then held: "Even if [officers] concocted a dubious scheme to bring about [the suspect's] arrest, it is the arrest itself and not the scheme that must be scrutinized for reasonableness under the Fourth Amendment."

In some states, state law is more restrictive of police authority to use force than is the federal constitutional standard. In others, the state standard may be looser – purporting to allow officers greater authority to use force than would the Constitution – and is therefore unconstitutional. Also possible is a mixture; state law may impose certain rules to which must be added one or more federal constitutional requirements. In any event, the starting point is to understand the federal constitutional standard. It establishes the baseline: No state law or agency policy may be more permissive than is the Constitution. Then, officers must consider whether their state law or agency policy creates higher – that is, more restrictive – standards which must be met as well. Of course, in most states, nothing prevents a plaintiff from also bringing a force claim under a state law tort theory alleging civil assault, battery, and wrongful death, as examples. Given federal constitutional law in this area, many plaintiffs' attorneys will do just that.

No state law or agency policy may be more permissive than is the Constitution.

Scenario #80 A police officer is in foot pursuit of a shoplifting suspect. While chasing the suspect, the officer observes a gun in the suspect's waistband. The officer then pulls out his gun and shouts, "Police! Stop or I'll shoot!"

Question: Is deadly force authorized at this point?

Answer: No. The crime for which the suspect is being pursued is not one that poses a serious physical threat to the officer or the public. The fact that he has a gun in his possession – which the suspect has not demonstrated an inclination to use – does not elevate this to a deadly force situation. The person is not "escaping by means of a deadly weapon" or otherwise presenting an imminent threat of death or serious injury.

Scenario #81 A police officer is involved in a physical altercation with a suspect who is resisting a lawful arrest. After struggling with the suspect unsuccessfully for two minutes, the officer is able to step back and fire an electronic control device, striking the suspect and causing him to fall to the ground. The suspect hits his head on the sidewalk and suffers a concussion. He later sues the officer because (he claims) the officer should have used his pepper spray, a lower level of force according to the officer's department's use of force policy. This would have, the suspect contends, prevented him from falling and hitting his head.

Question: Was the officer's use of force reasonable?

Answer: In all likelihood, yes. Assuming the suspect continued to pose a physical threat to the officer and remained combative, the use of the electronic control device was reasonable but so would have been the use of the pepper spray. The fact that the electronic control device amounted to a higher degree of force in the department's use of force policy does not necessarily make its use unreasonable. The officer is not required to incrementally increase his degree of force until he arrives at the level of force that accomplishes the desired goal. He is allowed to proceed directly to a level of force that reasonably relates to the threat presented and the goal of lawful control.

NOTES

[1] *See Scott v. Harris*, 550 U.S. 372 (2007), where the United States Supreme Court found a police ramming to end a dangerous high-speed pursuit was reasonable though it created a substantial risk of injury or death to the suspect.

[2] *See, for example, Forrett v. Richardson*, 112 F. 3d 416 (9th Cir. 1997).

A

Abandoned Property
  Expectation of privacy 158
    Garbage 159
    Vehicles 159
Airports
  Searches 143
Anonymous Tips 43, 135
  Search warrants 196
Arraignment
  Definition of 118
Arrests
  Discontinuation of arrest 25
  Involuntary movement of
    detainee 22
  Searches incident to 145
    Change of custody 148
    Vehicles 147
Arrest Warrant
  Definition of 89
Assertions Of Rights By Suspects 118
  Right to counsel 120
  Right to silence 120

B

Body Cavity Searches 148

C

Carroll Search 170
  Probable Cause 69
Cell Phones
  Searches incident to arrest 146
Checkpoints 57
Clear And Convincing Evidence 36
Coerced Statements 129
Community Caretaking
  Doctrine 88

Concerned Citizens
  Hearsay 40
Confidential Informants 42
Consent To Search
  Deception to obtain consent 181
  Rental property 183
  Vehicle stops 62
  Workplace searches 183
Crime Scenes
  Definition of 86
  Warrantless search 87
Criminal History
  Probable cause 48
Criminal Informants 41
Curtilage
  Definition of 156
Custody Principle
  Definition of 101
  Miranda Rule 100

D

Deadly Force 226
Discontinuation Of Arrest 25
Due Process Rights
  Lineups 216
  Non-testimonial identification 210

E

Electronic Eavesdropping
  Searches 175
Emergency Aid Exception
  Search warrant 88
Entry To Arrest
  Private premises 84
Entry To Preserve Evidence
  Private premises 86

Exigent Circumstances
   Definition of 83
   Officer-created exigencies 90
   Search of persons 141
      Strip and body cavity searches 148
   Search warrant requirements 141

F

Fifth Amendment
   Protection against self incrimination 115, 209
Fleeing Felon Rule 227
Forced Entry
   Definition of 81
   No-knock requirements 92
Fourth Amendment
   Non-testimonial identification 210
   Prohibition of searches and seizures 6, 115
   Reasonable search and seizure 223
   Search warrants 69
Free To Decline
   Voluntary contact 14
Free To Leave
   Inquiry 13
Frisks
   Carried articles 66
   Definition of 135
   Occupants of vehicles 65
   Reasonable suspicion 34
   Scope of 139
   Suspicion factors 137
   Vehicles 64
   Weapons 136
Fruit Of The Poisoned Tree 3, 22

G

Geographic Location Of Suspect
   Probable cause 45, 82
   Reasonable belief 82
GPS Tracking Devices
   Searches 175

H

Hearsay
   Concerned citizens 40
   Confidential informants 42
   Criminal informants 41
   Levels of 38
   Search warrants 194
   Sources of information 37

I

Identification Procedures
   Non-testimonial 209
Informants 41
   Confidential 42
   Criminal 41
Intent To Arrest
   Miranda warning 104
Interrogation
   Definition of 105
Inventory Searches
   Impoundment of vehicles 74
   Personal possessions of detainee 149
   Vehicle stops 74
Investigative Stops And Arrests 17, 102
   Expanding traffic stops 59
   Involuntary movement of detainee 21
   Probable cause 33
   Use of force and/or restraints 23

Involuntary Movement Of
   Detainee
   Arrest 22
   Investigative stop or arrest 21, 102

K

Knock And Announce
   Requirements
   Search warrants 92, 199

L

Lineups 213
   Due process rights 216
   Right to counsel 215

M

Media
   Execution of search warrants 202
Miranda Rights
   General requirements 99
   Right to counsel 116, 122
   Right to silence 117
   Waiver 16, 125
Miranda Rule
   14-Day Rule 122
   Custody test 26, 100
   Exceptions 110
   Right to counsel 115, 118
   Seizures 26
   State laws 100
   Voluntary contact 102
   Volunteered statements 111
Miranda v. Arizona 16
Miranda Waiver
   Definition of 108
Miranda Warning
   Definition of 100, 106

Intent to arrest 104
Interrogation 105
Re-warning 107
Terry stops 102
Voluntary contact 16
Model Code of Pre-Arraignment
   Criminal Procedure 3

N

Non-Testimonial Identification
   Procedures 209
   Due process rights 210
   Incident to arrest 210
   Juveniles 213
   State laws 210
   Uncooperativeness 218

O

Oath Of Office 3
Open Fields And Woods
   Searches 155

P

Person
   Seizure of 5
Photographic Arrays 213
Plain Feel Doctrine 140
Plain View Doctrine 140
   Definition of 167
   Vehicle stops 61, 75, 169
Pre-Arraignment Criminal
   Procedure 3
Preponderance Of The Evidence 36
Privacy, Expectation Of
   Abandoned property 158
   Curtilage 156
   Garbage 159
   Open fields and woods 155

Sensory enhancement tools 173
Vehicles 62
Private Premises 86
　Entry to arrest 84
　Entry to preserve evidence 86
　Exigent circumstances 83
　Protective sweeps 94
Private Schools
　Searches 143
Probable Cause
　Anonymous tips 43
　Carroll search 69
　Collective knowledge 51
　Criminal history 48
　Definition of 33
　Description similarities 47
　Discontinuation of arrest 25
　Establishment of 34
　Geographic location of suspect 45
　High crime area 45
　Investigative stops and arrests 33
　Observed behaviors 47
　Profiling 49
　Searches and seizures 6, 33, 141, 145
　Search of private premises 81
　Search warrants 196
　Sensory perception 46, 171
　Sources of information 37
　Stopping a vehicle 57
　Time factor 46
　To arrest 34
　To search 34
　To seize 34
　Weapons frisk 33
Profiling
　Probable cause 49

Proof Beyond A Reasonable Doubt 36
Property
　Seizure of 5
Protective Sweeps 201
　Private premises 94
　Reasonable suspicion 34, 94

R

Reasonable Belief
　Discussion of 82
Reasonable Suspicion
　Collective knowledge 51
　Criminal history 48
　Definition of 33
　Establishment of 34
　Expanding traffic stops 59
　Frisks 135
　Non-custodial identification orders 211
　Profiling 49
　Protective sweeps 34, 94, 201
　Sensory perception 46
　Sources of information 37
　Stopping a vehicle 57
　Time factor 46
　To frisk 34
　Vehicle checkpoints 57
　Voluntary contact 11
Right To Counsel
　Assertion of rights 120
　Identification process 215
　Lineups 215
　Miranda rights 116, 118, 122
　Sixth Amendment 115
　Waiver of rights 125
Right To Silence
　Assertion of rights 120
　Fifth Amendment 117
　Miranda rights 117

S

Schools
  Searches 142
    Private schools 143
Searches
  Abandoned property 158
  Airport 143
  Body cavity searches 148
  Consent to search 181
  Curtilage 156
  Definiton of 4
  Electronic eavesdropping 175
  Frisks 135
  Garbage 159
  GPS tracking devices 175
  Incident to arrest 141, 145
    Cell phones 146
    Change of custody 148
    Non-testimonial evidence 210
    Scope of 146
    Vehicles 147
  Inventory of detainee's possessions 149
  Open fields and woods 155
  Probable cause 34
    Sensory perceptions 171
  Probationers and parolees 144
  Schools 142
  Sensory enhancement tools 173
  Sensory perceptions 171
  Strip searches 148
  Workplace searches 183
Search And Seizure
  Non-testimonial identification 210
Search Warrants
  Benefits of 192
  Care of evidence 203
  Corroboration 196
  Crime scene 87
  Definition of 192
  Emergency aid doctrine 88
  Execution of 197
    Detaining persons present 200
    Searches of persons present 201
  Exigent circumstances 141
  Hearsay 194
  Jurisdictional issues 198
  Knock, announce and wait requirements 92, 199
  Length of search 203
  Media involvement 202
  Obtaining the warrant 197
  Probable cause statements 194, 196
  School searches 142
  Securing the premises 203
  State laws 191
  Time frames 198
  Vehicle stops 69
Seizures
  Definiton of 5, 193
  Free to leave inquiry 13
  Length of investigative stop 17
  Miranda Rule 26
  Plain View Doctrine 167
  Probable cause 34
    Sensory perceptions 171
  Voluntary contact 11
Sensory Perception
  Probable cause 46, 171
Show-Ups 217
Sixth Amendment
  Miranda rights 105
  Right to counsel 115
    Assertion of rights 120

Identification process 215
Non-testimonial
  identification 210
Sources Of Information
  Concerned citizens 40
  Credibility 39
  Hearsay 37
  Probable cause 37
  Reasonable suspicion 37
State Laws 3
  Electronic eavesdropping 175
  Miranda Rule 100
  Non-testimonial identification
    210
  Return of search warrants 203
  Search warrants 191
  Use of force 233
Strip Searches 148

T

Terry Stops 11, 17, 23, 26, 65,
    102, 135
  Miranda warning 102

U

Unarrest 25
Uncooperativeness
  Probable cause 50
Use Of Force
  Deadly force 226
  Investigative stops and arrests
    23
  Less lethal force 231
  Reasonableness 225
  State laws 233
  To prevent escape 229
  Warning 227

V

Vehicle Checkpoints 57
Vehicle Searches
  Incident to arrest 147
  Plain View Doctrine 169
Vehicle Stops
  Carroll search 69
  Consent to search 62
  Expectation of privacy 62
  Frisk of occupants 65
  Inventory searches 74
  Plain View Doctrine 61
  Pretextual stops 58
  Search incident to arrest of
    occupant 67
  Stopping a vehicle 57
  Weapons frisk 64
Voluntary Contact 11
  Free to decline test 14
  Miranda warning 16, 102
Voluntary Statements 129

W

Warrants
  Arrest warrants 89
  Warrantless entry 84
Warrantless Entry 84
  Crime scenes 87
  Officer created exigency 90
Warrantless Seizure 140
Weapons Frisks 136
  Probable cause 33